Christians In Crisis:

Debt Centered Crisis, Christ Centered Solution

Christians In Crisis:

Debt Centered Crisis, Christ Centered Solution

Steven Cohen, Esq.

Christians In Crisis:

Debt Centered Crisis, Christ Centered Solution

© Steven Cohen 2018

This book is a work of fiction. Named locations are used fictitiously, and characters and incidents are the product of the author's imagination. Any resemblance to actual events or places or persons, living or dead, is entirely coincidental.

All rights reserved. Without limiting the rights under copyright reserved above, no part of this publication may be reproduced, stored in a retrieval system, or transmitted, in any form or by any means (electronic, mechanical, photocopying, recording or otherwise), without the prior written permission of the copyright owner of this book.

Published by
Lighthouse Christian Publishing
SAN 257-4330
5531 Dufferin Drive
Savage, Minnesota, 55378
United States of America

www.lighthousechristianpublishing.com

Table of Contents

Prologue	Introduction of Hope
Chapter 1	How did I get into all this debt?
Chapter 2	You have to have *change* to get out of debt.
Chapter 3	The Four *Musts* of Debt Freedom
Chapter 4	Becoming Debt Savvy
Chapter 5	Your Mortgage
Chapter 6	Student Loans
Chapter 7	Car Loans
Chapter 8	Discretionary Purchases
Chapter 9	Dead Weight Debt
Chapter 10	Credit Cards
Chapter 11	Medical Bills
Chapter 12	Judgments and Suits
Chapter 13	Bankruptcy
	Chapter 7
	Chapter 13
Chapter 14	Foreclosures
Chapter 15	Crisis Management 101
	Their Plan
	Your Plan
Chapter 16	Financial Management 101
Chapter 17	Is there a Heavenly 401 K plan?
Chapter 18	Run to Win the Race to debt freedom

Dedication

This book and its caring devotion to the readers who read it's text is dedicated to my loving wife Susie and my sweet daughters Christy and Kaitlyn; all of whom brighten my life each day.

Introduction of Hope

> You make known to me the path of life; you will fill me with joy in your presence, with eternal pleasures at your right hand."
>
> Palms 16:11

In my legal practice dealing with bankruptcies and debt defense, I have seen so many fine families drowning in debt over the last fifteen years. Both Christians and non-Christians alike face a tough world where debt is common, mercy is rare, and an ultimate solution can seem impossible. Yet there is a way out of this seemingly unsolvable debt crisis which so many of God's people face. With an eye toward the wisdom of Solomon, the steadfastness of Job and the merciful example of our Lord, I have written this text to give guidance and hope to those in and approaching a debt crisis. With dedication, faith and a new heart and attitude toward spending and debt, there is a way out and a solution for everyone willing to take the needed steps toward debt freedom. As a believer and an attorney, it has anguished me to see so many individuals and families drowning in their debt. Most, through no fault of their own, have found themselves caught in the thistles and thorns of debt. Debt crisis is a progression which creeps up on the seemingly unsuspecting. Its causes are numerous, some avoidable and some not: the failure to budget, a lost job, reduced work, a repossessed car, an increased mortgage payment, credit cards and the list of reasons and excuses goes on and on.

Our country was built on liberty, freedom and the pursuit of happiness, the principals of religious freedom and equal protection under the law. Slavery was abolished and we have come a long way in overcoming the evils of bias and prejudice. However, we have a new adversary which has overcome us and it is as menacing as the fiercest disease. Its Debt! Debt is both a taskmaster and a contagious illness. It has overtaken all facets of our lives and lurks around every corner. Home loans, car loans, credit cards, personal loans, bills for cell phones, cable, health insurance, day care, furniture, clothes, food and the list goes on and on in perpetuity. What happened to prosperity in America? It has been packaged and sold to others in the form of our debt. We live in a world where getting into debt is encouraged at every corner and with every ad an irresistible offer; however, beware to you who do not repay, as there is no mercy in the land and no creditor willing to forgive us our debts like our Lord and Savior, Jesus!

The burden and stress of this life have become so overwhelming, so complex and so seemingly unsolvable. Where do we go? What do we do? How do we get out of debt? This book will explain the Where, When and How; and with an eye on Christ as our supreme guide, seek to explain the Why. This text will give you back the keys to secure your financial future and offer a guide, complete with detailed steps to procuring the solution to the seemingly unsolvable state that so many Christians find themselves in, a state of debt crisis.

We are a nation engulfed in debt. The pyramids of Egypt are and were truly a wonder beyond comprehension, but their size and impressiveness are dwarfed by the incredulous size of this nation's debt. Our nation's stimulus plan passed in 2009 was some $787 billion dollars. Let's look at that number: $787,000,000,000. That's basically spending just over $2600 a person for each of the approximately 300 million people in the U.S and to make matters worse it was all on credit. If a hundred thousand slaves were used to build all the Egyptian pyramids over 5,000 years ago, our stimulus plan could have paid each of them almost 8 million in today's dollars. Looking at those numbers, it would be incredulous to imagine that we're not a nation drowning in debt.

When Moses led the nation of Israel out of slavery in Egypt, who would have thought that God's people, both Jew and Gentile, Christian and non Christian, would one day willingly submit to slavery. This new type of slavery, debt slavery, is self imposed over a period of time, and is certainly a form of indentured servitude. We have indentured ourselves and sold ourselves to our creditors as debtors. Unwittingly, Christians along with the rest of the nation have been lured into complacency with our ever increasing level of debt. Purchase after purchase plus seemingly low payment after low payment equals higher and higher interest. Yes, there is a new form of slavery in modern America. Its victims are many and slow to realize their indentured state until it is almost too late. As Christians face mounting debts, the church faces a great burden as well, maintaining its vital outreach in a season when their donors are already overextended.

It is not too late; however, there is hope even for the seemingly hopeless. Remember, this is America and it is the land of opportunity. There are many ways to get into debt, but there are also numerous ways to get out of debt and that is the goal of this book, to start you well on your way to debt freedom. Let's see how many links there are in the chain of debt that you have been making over the years. If your chain is not yet formed, then take this book as a practical guide to live by, to form a debt free and prosperous future. Too many people have no clue the trouble they are in until it seems too late. As you take account of your assets and liabilities, you will be able to determine just how much trouble you are really in; but you will also see how you can be set free from the burden of debt with Christ as your cornerstone.

CHAPTER 1

How did I get into all this debt?

> Keep your lives free from the love of money and be content with what you have, because God has said, "Never will I leave you; never will I forsake you."
>
> Hebrews 13:5 NIV

"But I had such great credit!" This is a term I have heard more times than I can count by those drowning in debt. "Credit" has become a modern day rock star or idol if you will. Credit drives the rate we are offered, the amount we can be loaned, and our status as borrowers in the credit community. However, like so many things, credit can be abused, albeit unwittingly, to the point of self destruction. Having credit does not mean that you can afford to pay back the amount you're loaned, but simply that someone is willing to loan you the money, sometimes at astonishingly high rates of interest. We know that the Lord will never leave us nor forsake us; however, we also know that there may be times of trouble. From both the book of Job in the Old Testament and Matthew in the New Testament, we know that he "sends rain on the righteous and the unrighteous" Matthew 5:45 NIV; difficult times will be experienced by both the person who plans well and the person who is careless. Job was "...blameless and upright" Job 1:1 NIV, yet he still suffered tremendous family and financial loss. You may be asking yourself, "How did I get into all this debt? Is there any solution? Was I not serving God? Why did things not work out for me? Why am I giving more to the credit card companies in interest than I am to the church in my tithe?" The verses scribed at the beginning of this chapter are just a few among so many beautiful and encouraging verses we find in the scriptures. For years I have dealt with families and friends in financial crisis. With the bursting of the real estate bubble, I saw some of the finest and kindest people suffer tremendous losses. A financial famine has overtaken the land; and God's people have once again gone from enjoying the years of plenty to pondering uncertainty during these years of want. For most, there is no grain in the storehouse; it has been sold, borrowed against or mortgaged away.

  The book of Job has given us an important and permanent example that one's own spirituality may have no relation to the crisis at hand. Financial and family losses are a reality of this life and a result of sin in general and not necessarily sin of a particular individual or family. The book of Job also shows the great folly in judging others and in coming to any negative conclusion as to the sufferings of others.

So how did you get here? In debt? In trouble? Or on the verge of a financial meltdown? It's not hard and it is almost the same story retold from one family to the next, over and over again. It's not a lack of education or of a poor moral upbringing; quite the contrary, it's the result of a culture built almost entirely on the concept of credit, buying now and paying later. Stretching ourselves financially thin is further buttressed by the media and a constant bombardment of ads, pushing the mantra of having it all now with no burden attached of future planning.

A Typical Family's Progression into Debt

So how does it start? It starts with an ordinary couple or individual who wants a home. They find a great one and buy the home shortly after making their loan application and getting approved for their first truly large loan. For sake of example, Mr. and Mrs. Homebuyer take out an $180,000 mortgage with about a $1600 monthly payment. The payments are within their grasp, but soon it's time for a new car. The car has all the right features and at $25,000 with a payment of $450 a month, they're still alright.   But what would a house be without furniture? As a homeowner, their credit rating is great and the furniture is all neatly put on credit for another $6000 in debt. The payments on credit start low but Mr. and Mrs. Homebuyer soon realize that they need to send in $175 a month to try and really work their debt down. Here's how our sample family looks so far:

Family Debt Stage: 1

Debt	Payment	
$180,000	$1600	House
$ 25,000	$ 450	Car
$ 6,000	$ 175	Furniture
------------	------------	
$211,000 Total	$2225	Monthly Payments

Well a few years later, Mr. and Mrs. Homebuyer have a child and that bundle of joy requires that a few more bundles be purchased. Marketing to their needs, credit card companies send out several offers, and the proud parents suddenly have $20,000 of available credit. They don't use it all, of course, but do build up about $10,000 in credit card debt which they can still pay pretty easily by making minimum payments. Our happy couple figures they will pay it off later. Next, one car is not enough for the growing family and since work is going well, they buy a luxury car for $30,000 and add a $600 monthly car payment to the equation. The wife now wants to expand her horizons and is going to school and incurring student loans. Before you know it, the deferred bill for student loans is $20,000. Just as their family has expanded, their home value has increased, so they take out a $35,000 second mortgage and have a new $400 monthly loan payment. Now Mr. and Mrs. Homebuyer's finances look like the equation below, although they are personally too busy to keep track:

Family Debt Stage: 2

Debt	Payment	
$180,000	$1600	House
$ 25,000	$ 450	Car
$ 6,000	$ 175	Furniture
$ 30,000	$ 600	Car 2
$ 10,000	$ 300	Credit Card
$ 40,000	$ 400	2nd Mortgage
$ 20,000	deferred	Student Loans
------------	------------	
$311,000 Total	$3525	Monthly Payments

This all too common problem now becomes twofold. First, the family encounters an unexpected job loss or a cut back on overtime pay at work. Second, with no financial plan in place, the family has not budgeted any flexibility or savings into their monthly bills. They are living on the edge of their ability, meaning that with any additional strain or problem, Mr. and Mrs. Homebuyer go from living well to living in crisis. Suddenly, they can barely make their car payments and, what's worse; they start adding debt to their credit cards. Because they have a history of being such good payers, Mr. and Mrs. Homebuyer now have $35,000 of available credit; and they start using it just to pay the bills. The credit card companies love the business, but all the zero percent interest rate offers are over because that's just bait to get you hooked; their rates are on the rise and Mr. and Mrs. Homebuyer are paying interest rates between 19% and 25% for their credit cards. The ability or even desire to pay down the cards becomes secondary as paying the mortgage and cars take priority. When the family finally takes time to sit down at the kitchen table and add up their credit cards and bills, the phone rings. Their daughter answers and says, "There is a rude man on the phone asking when are we going to pay our bill and threatening to take us to court." Frustrated, a monthly list of expenses and bills is scribbled down only to be interrupted by another call from a collector informing them that another card is overdue. For the next few months, the family trades off what bills to pay and tries not to answer the phone until there is a knock on the door from a process server with a foreclosure lawsuit. The mortgage is now three months overdue and all the credit cards are in default. What we find here is a Christian in crisis.

CHAPTER 2

You have to have *change* to get out of debt!

> Therefore, if anyone is in Christ, the new creation has come: The old has gone, the new is here!
> 2 Corinthians 5:17 NIV

Not only do you need *change* in your pocket to buy that cafe latte, but you need *change* in your life to get out of debt. A born again Christian undergoes a change in their life upon accepting Christ, the old things have passed away and there is a new way of living. Old lifestyles and sinful habits are left at the door.

What about money and how we deal with it? The Bible gives the example of a good steward and a bad steward of money, Mathew 25:14-28 NIV. The one that hid what was given to him and failed to make it grow had what little he had taken away. So what if your funds are hidden or, worse yet, you're so overextended that you are in great debt? Well, first off, don't worry; you're not alone. Second, there is still time to be a good steward, even a great one, but you must change your ways. The example of the good steward also shows that different people are entrusted with different levels of funds, referred to in the Bible as a "talent" or a measure of gold, Exodus 37:24 NIV. Whether you have a small income or a great income, few or many "talents", you must utilize them wisely. Remember the woman whom Jesus noticed in the temple giving just one coin. She had little, but she spent it wisely and will be immortalized in the scriptures for her sacrificial gift. A wisely placed investment can pay handsomely, but so can a wisely saved or unspent dollar.

The spending habits of those drowning in debt can typically be generalized as unplanned and without control. The individual bordering on bankruptcy is not carefully calculating his monthly car payment to determine what he can afford before going to the dealer. It's a complete afterthought. You don't get into twelve, twenty, fifty or even one hundred thousand dollars in credit card debt when you have a financial plan. You get into that kind of debt when your eyes and emotions control what you buy and not your income. Over the years, I have had hundreds of discussions with families in financial trouble and I have yet to have one pull out a budget and say, "This is the budget which I have been operating under for the last few years, and I just don't know what went wrong." No, most people in financial trouble haven't been operating on a budget. Certainly there are the exceptions to the rule. Quite a wide variety of factors can lead a person into financial trouble and some of those are just out of one's control. A lost job, a failing business, a health crisis, an unexpected natural disaster affecting one's home or a broken marriage are just a few of the unplanned events which can trigger a financial crisis in spite of good planning. What this book will attempt to do, whatever your situation, is to jump start you toward debt freedom, toward a new you and a new way of thinking about debt, enabling you to escape from the financial crisis at hand. But it all starts with having *change*. *Change* in the way you look at your finances. *Change* in the way you make decisions about purchases. *Change* in how you manage your money. Serious change will bring serious results. If you're in financial trouble and choose to continue down the same path, you are likely headed to destruction, or at least financial destruction. So get ready to change your ways! A little change in your life and in how you operate will eventually put change in the right place, your pocket.

CHAPTER 3

The Four *Musts* of Debt Freedom

You must take control of your finances if you want to get out of debt! Your old ways of paying your bills, buying and spending have to end. Random purchases, with no rhyme or reason, must end in favor of a preplanned budget with a set spending limit. The way you use to operate is over. Don't say "but this is how I do it" because that rationale landed you in your present crisis. The old method was the road to nowhere. You need a new way of operating, a new way of spending and a new way of saving. When Jesus forgave a sinner, he would add an admonishment, "Stop sinning" John 5:14 NIV. He would cure and give directions on how to stay cured, how to live and how to have a happy life. To escape the debt trap, you must change and become a new financial creature. I have lost count of how many families I have spoken with who couldn't answer two basic (essential) questions: How much do you earn? How much do you owe? If you can't answer both questions without pulling out your paycheck and bills, you're already in trouble. Imagine asking a pilot before a flight, "How far can this plane fly on a tank of gas?" and hearing him say, "Well I don't know." Getting nervous, you should be. How can a pilot safely fly a plane if he or she can't answer such a basic question?   The same comparison applies to money. How can you successfully manage your own finances if you can't answer the two most basic financial questions regarding your income and your debts? The answer is you can't, and that's why **you must take control of your finances.**

Second, **you must be debt savvy.** You have to realize that there are number crunchers out there working day and night to devour you. Satan devours the weak, but the lenders devour the uninformed and uncaring. You have to start thinking about debt as your enemy and as a hindrance to your future. How can you fully serve the Lord if your every second is consumed with creditors calling on you to pay your bills? Both you and I have given the credit card companies $39 for a late fee far many more times then we arbitrarily gave $39 in the offering. The Lord doesn't charge a late fee if you miss the offering but your credit card company does. In fact, they are counting on you to mismanage your money as a way to pad their own pockets.

> No one can serve two masters. Either you will hate the one and love the other, or you will be devoted to the one and despise the other. You cannot serve both God and money.
>
> Matthew 6:24 NIV

This book is going to try and make you debt savvy and help you to think about debt in a whole new light. Debt should not be your master. But how can you effectively escape the slippery slope that lands you in a pile of debt? Part of becoming debt savvy is not just keeping a box of bills and aimlessly acknowledging its existence. Many a client has come in with their bills in a box. A box is where you throw trash, not your money.

How you spend your money is equally important to how you earn it. We have all heard that Jesus said, "It is more blessed to give than to receive" as related to us in Acts 20:35 NIV. But as my father, a former minister, would constantly say, "It's better to be able to give then to need to receive." Wouldn't it be nice to be able to give? Do you know how much you owe? Do you know what interest rates you are being charged? Do you know how long it will take you to pay off your bills? **Start** knowing. **Start** understanding. Empty that box of bills onto your table and take it seriously. Make your list of debts, interest rates, monthly payments and become debt savvy. Do you truly understand what is happening when you make a purchase and incur more debt? Do you really know the cost of what you are buying? If you earn $15 an hour and buy a meal for $15, you have traded one hour of your time for the meal. That's okay, but now let's put it on a credit card. When you charge that same $15, you have said, "I promise to work one hour for that meal." But wait, if you're paying 20% interest on that card, the amount of time you have agreed to work to pay it off is increasing each month. Take two years to pay off that meal and now you owe an hour and a half, and so on, and so on. What about a bigger purchase? For example, if you buy something for $1500, you have said "I'll work

100 hours to pay it off"; put it on your credit card and a year later it will take you 120 hours to pay it off. What you have to start saying to yourself before a purchase is, "How will I pay this off and when?" and "Do I have the money for this purchase in my budget?" It may not be fun to ask yourself such contemplative questions, but it's a whole lot better then spending 120 hours working to pay off something you bought a year ago or 144 hours to pay off something you bought 2 years ago.

Wait a minute, what if you are operating below your budget, instead of over budget, and you have $1500 in savings? Then you could make the purchase in cash and not have to work any more to pay it off. This strategy is the eventual ideal plan. If you operate out of savings and surplus, you won't be playing catch up. To truly become debt savvy, you must understand and know your debts, master them and not let them be the master of you.

Third, **you must trust God**. Don't get discouraged about the amount of debt you're in; just start working toward a solution and trust God. Thankfully there is no debtor's prison in the United States, so whether your $5,000 in debt or $500,000 in debt, it's all paperwork, albeit expensive paperwork. Jesus certainly wasn't concerned with earthly needs as was evident in the reply he gave in the book of Matthew:

> Jesus replied, "Foxes have dens and birds have nests, but the Son of Man has no place to lay his head."
>
> Matthew 8:20 NIV

Jesus also encouraged his disciples in Matthew 17:20 with the admonition that if they had the faith of a mustard seed, they could move mountains. Almost nothing can seem more impossible then a mountain of debt. But then, nothing is impossible for God. Look for the silver lining within your situation. Do you know the Lord? Then you have what is most important. You may have suffered a foreclosure and feel that all is lost, but it may have been a blessing in disguise. That overwhelming mortgage debt that you were struggling so desperately to pay is typically ended with a foreclosure. If it's behind you, it's time to move forward toward debt freedom and the peace that comes with it.

Fourth, **you must have a budget**. I can't emphasize enough the importance of a budget to your financial future. It's critical, and if you took nothing else from this book other than working from a budget, you would discover the prospect of financial freedom lies within your grasp. Virtually no one in overwhelming credit card debt has operated off of a budget. If they did, they would have long ago realized the disastrous situation they were in, and corrective measures would have been implemented. A good budget will immediately set limits on spending, create a payoff plan for debts and provide a course of savings for the future. A good budget can also help facilitate that too often overlooked tithe that can be bridging your ministry into the future and God's blessings into the present.

One of my many questions to clients when discussing debt is, "Do you have a plan?" I refuse to let them settle with just an "I think" or "I will", but I insist on bringing them to the point of an affirmative answer to, "Do you have a written plan to get out of debt?" The Bible is God's ultimate plan for our life. The future of God's kingdom has been clearly laid out in a plan in the book of Revelation. We have been given a limited time on this earth; therefore, we should also carefully plan what we are doing with the time with which we have been entrusted in addition to how we will use and manage the resources we have been given.

CHAPTER 4

Becoming Debt Savvy

> Let the wise listen and add to their learning, and let the discerning get guidance— for understanding proverbs and parables, the sayings and riddles of the wise. The fear of the LORD is the beginning of knowledge, but fools despise wisdom and instruction.
> Proverbs 1:5-7 NIV

Are you debt savvy? You know your A B C's but do you know the A B C's about debt? If not, you better start learning because your creditors spend day and night analyzing the numbers and studying how to make more money. More of your money! Remember, every dollar you've paid in interest over the years has gone into someone else's pocket. Not all debt is the same, however, and not all debtors are as profitable to their creditors as others. Who is the most profitable debtor to the creditor? The least informed, the least concerned, the least knowledgeable. While you're too busy, too preoccupied with life's difficulties and struggles, the creditor is cashing in big time. Cashing in on late fees, high interest rates and over-the-limit fees. Ever heard of any classes given by credit card companies to educate the consumer? I haven't. I have heard of businesses set up to help you pay them their money.

Not all debt is the same. Debt comes in many different forms, some good, some bad and some plain old devastating. What causes people to topple are the bad and the devastating debt they have incurred that boomerangs back towards them, and this debt is often the proverbial straw that breaks the camel's back. Sadly, many consumers know they shouldn't succumb to even one more purchase, but in a moment of weakness, that one additional debt puts them over the edge. If they had only studied their situation a little more. If they had only understood where they were—that they were already on the brink of disaster. So many people don't realize that they are already in trouble, already far beyond the boundaries of where they should be financially. Just because you can make your payments right now doesn't mean you're in a good position or that you're not in trouble.

So let's look at some different types and categories of debt. The first step to debt freedom is to understand where you are financially, what types of debt you have, what types of debt you need to avoid like the plague and what types of debts you just have to get rid of. I like to break them up into three main categories: Long Term, Short Term and Luxury/High Interest Debts:

LONG TERM DEBT (10 Years or more)

HOME: Mortgage(s)

EDUCATIONAL: Student Loan(s)

Your job, on average, is designed to generate enough income to pay one mortgage, one car loan and normal bills such as utilities, groceries and the like. It's when you start overloading your income that you start encountering problems. Once you're overloaded, if anything goes out of balance, the whole thing goes. For most, it is the dead weight debts that are their eventual undoing. Dead weight is a term used for items that bear no fruit, no benefit. Dead weight debt is like overeating bacon and fat. It eventually catches up with you and can instigate a debt heart attack.

We will look at each type of debt and the concept behind maintaining them, one at a time in the chapters that follow. The first debt, a home mortgage, falls under the long-term debt category and is the most common and reasonable of the debts discussed.

CHAPTER 5

Your Mortgage

> Others were saying, "We are mortgaging our fields, our vineyards and our homes to get grain during the famine."
>
> Nehemiah 5:3 NIV

Does the above verse sound familiar? Mortgages and overwhelming debt were a sign of the times in more than just our generation. A home mortgage is the single largest debt you will incur during your lifetime and the single largest monthly payment you will make. Mortgages typically range from 15 to 30 years in length, and they are long term loans to say the least. One avenue to personal wealth, if not simply financial security, is to pay off your mortgage. Although it's easier said than done, it's not impossible. Paying off your home mortgage is a matter of planning, making additional principal payments and tenacity. It's also a matter of sticking with your first home until it's paid off. Each time your mortgage is refinanced, the clock starts ticking again for the new loan term, 15 to 30 years. Each time your home is sold and a new one purchased, the clock starts again, 15 to 30 years. You can soon see how valuable it would be to remain in the same home for a long time. If you could stick it out and, better yet, add funds each month to your mortgage payment, you could shorten the span by many years, eventually enjoying years with no mortgage payments. Imagine starting a 15 year mortgage payment at age 25 and being done at age 40. Time goes quicker than you think and the rewards are great for those who can brave it out. A surprising fact is that the additional cost to make a 30 year mortgage a 15 year mortgage is not so great. The sad fact is that those who take on a mortgage beyond their ability are gambling with disaster.

Home ownership is both rewarding and satisfying, and the interest you pay can be a tax deductible expense. In good times, homes are an appreciating asset. In bad times, only those that budgeted and planned can survive. What happens however, when we bite off more than we can chew? A hefty mortgage can be a menacing chain that can exhaust our dearest resources to no end. We will look at mortgages from both sides: First, Where to start? Second, What if I'm already in over my head and in foreclosure?

When buying or refinancing a home you need to keep some basic premises in mind. First, the expense has to be budgeted and you need a grip on what you can and cannot afford from your budget. When you are applying for a loan to buy or refinance a home, the question should not be "How much will they lend me?" It must be, "How much can I comfortably afford?" I use the word "comfortably" because I'm trying to keep you out of trouble, by not placing you on the edge of your financial capabilities. The edge is where you are without a financial plan and that's not where you will ever go again once you have a sensible budget. Remember, loans are like indentured servitude; so consider carefully how much debt you are getting yourself into as you soberly keep in mind that you are the one that's going to be paying the bill. You have to make a careful evaluation of your own income and expenses in determining whether or not you can comfortably afford the home.

Types of Home Loans

Fixed vs. Variable

With so many loan types, how do I know what's right for me? The answer may be simpler than you think and it lies within the budget itself. The need for certainty and reliability can only be met with a fixed rate loan. To be fixed means to be immovable and unchanging. That's what you want your payment to be, immovable, certain and without a doubt. The problem with variable rates is in planning for the increase payment. Almost no one plans for it and then the surge comes in; what seemed to be years down the road hits hard and fast. Another problem with variable rates is they generally always increase in the future. The increase is as good as having a salary reduction and that is of no help to anyone's budget. Hybrid loans are a mixture of the two, sometimes called 5/1 arms and various other names. These types of loans are fixed for a period of years, let's say 5 years, and they become variable. Sounds good up front, but what if you have a real estate bubble burst at the end of the five years. Suddenly, all those people who planned to refinance can't refinance. I don't like any loan that has a timeline attached to it. I'm not saying that arms can never be good or that you can't use it to your financial advantage. I am saying that for the typical consumer who does not plan in advance, a loan which will have a substantial increase in its payment in five years can pose a problem.

100% Financing

(Mortgage Insurance and 80/20 Loans)

If you put less than 20% down on your next home purchase you will likely be introduced to mortgage insurance. Mortgage insurance is a modern day invention and it protects the bank against your own default in the terms of your loan. It is for the most part lost money and the payment on MIP (Mortgage Insurance Premium) can range from a few dollars to many hundreds of dollars per month. To overcome the need for mortgage insurance, lenders started offering an 80/20 loan. An 80/20 loan is a two mortgage loan designed to overcome the need for MIP by having a first mortgage for 80% of the home's value and a second mortgage for the other 20% of the home's value. The 80/20 loan thus solved two problems for those buying homes. First, it eliminated the need for MIP. Second, it allowed buyers to purchase with no money down, i.e. 100% financing. The first mortgage would be for 80% of the home's value and therefore no mortgage insurance would be required. The second mortgage would be for the remaining 20% of the home's value, at typically a much higher interest rate. Sounds great, except now you've borrowed every cent so your debt is greater and you have a higher rate on top of it. You see with an 80/20 you're starting off with two mortgages and a higher rate charged by the bank. Obviously, this is not the preferred way to go and if you do go here, you need to have a lot of room in your budget. You also need to aggressively work to eliminate the second mortgage because that is where a lot of homeowners come into trouble during tough times.

Home Equity Lines

Home equity lines of credit are like second mortgages with a credit card attached. You can keep them for an emergency or simply run up the tab. The problem with home equity lines is that they are secured loans, meaning they are attached to your home, and they are increasing the length of time it will take to pay off your home. If you can avoid them, stay away. If you have one, work to pay it off and don't increase the balance any more. Remember each debt is a progression into trouble. Your financial machine, you, is designed for one home mortgage, not two.

Second Mortgages

Second mortgages are like home equity lines, however, they are taken out all at once. The second mortgage company can foreclose on your home just like the first mortgage can if the loan is in default. This is a second tier debt and an extra debt, a luxury debt, meaning you don't need it. If you can avoid a second mortgage, avoid it. This is the type of loan you take out for an operation on your child, not for a luxury purchase or for a home that you can't really afford. If you don't have the money to buy what you're looking at, then don't buy it. Save your money until you have enough of a down payment to avoid needing a second. You may say, "I'm buying a home and the only way I can afford it is with a second mortgage." This book is focused on getting you out of debt. A second mortgage is another long term debt, meaning one that you will have to pay on for years and years. Second mortgages also typically have higher rates of interest which means they are more costly and take more of your income away from you. What if I came to you and said I need an extra $275 a month from you for 30 years; that's in essence what a second mortgage does. So save your money and you can be earning the interest instead of the bank.

Interest Only Loans

I have no interest in any interest only loans! Why? Interest only is like a leased mortgage. With a lease, you make payments during a period of time and then turn back the property to its owner. You gain no ownership interest or equity; you simply have the use of the item or property. Interest only is like leasing the money. After 10 years of interest only payments, you owe the exact same amount as when you started. If you're paying interest only on your loan, you're going nowhere fast. You're on a treadmill of debt. You're working endlessly for the creditor and you're virtually a slave to the debt. You must budget some additional principal payments into your budget, **now!** An interest only loan is also symptomatic of financial trouble. When all you can maintain is the debt service on your debts, you're likely operating like our government, at a deficit. This is not a good financial state to be in, because there is no clock ticking on getting you out of debt. With interest only, you're in financial trouble, whether you know it or not. Interest only is not financial planning, it's a delay tactic and a ticket to nowhere. Get out of it now! How can I get out of an interest only loan? It may be much simpler than you think. Most interest only loans can be easily turned into 10, 15 and 30 year loans by simply adding an additional payment each month towards principal. You would simply mail in a payment marked "principal payment" to your lender each month. Work out a spread sheet with the current balance and interest rate. Play with the numbers and see how much you can shorten it by adding in a principal payment. Then check your balance each month to make sure it's being credited correctly. If it's automatically deducted, you may be able to set the additional principal payments up through your lender. Don't just assume it's all going right, check your statement each month and get excited about the reduced balance. It will pay off handsomely sooner then you think.

Reverse Mortgages

Doesn't *reverse* mean *backwards*? That's the direction you're going with a reverse mortgage, backwards. Hey, you're going the wrong way! The balance increases during the life of the loan, not decreases; and it's typically only offered to older homeowners to help them cope with a fixed stream of income. The benefit of a reverse mortgage is that the payments are made from your home's equity, not your bank account. But wait, it's still your money and it's being paid, as real as real can be, from your home's equity. The bank makes the loan with an anticipated payback down the road. That road typically ends when you die. Many reverse mortgaged properties are lost to foreclosure when the homeowner dies. If the beneficiaries of an estate with a reverse mortgage don't have the ability to pay off the mortgage or to sell it in short order, then the home will be lost to foreclosure. Mix this complexity with our recent real estate bubble and declining home values and it's a recipe for disaster. It's not a disaster for the homeowner, but it can be for their heirs who had hoped to retain the home.

Why doesn't the bank tell you all this at closing? Well they probably do, but it's within those 50 to 100 pages of documents being signed at the closing within about 30 minutes. It's certainly something that should be discussed with your children beforehand, and there should be a clear exit plan in place before a reverse mortgage is ever taken out.

As with all closings, it pays to have an attorney present to explain what's going on and what the pros and cons are. If your goal is for your family to have your home and for it to be around for many years, then a reverse mortgage may not be a good choice. If you have no heirs, can't move, and simply must reduce your monthly costs, then it may fit the bill.

Refinancing

Over the years, I have conducted hundreds of closings. Here are ten guiding rules when buying or refinancing a home; but, please remember that the goal of this book is to get you out of debt and to help you avoid bad debts. So let's set up a future of plenty, not of want:

---

10 GUIDING RULES WHEN BUYING OR REFINANCING

---

1. **How much can you borrow?**

There are many formulas for determining how much one can borrow when buying or refinancing a home; however, the simplest and best formula to follow is your own budget. Let your budget be your guide. If it doesn't work on paper, it doesn't work. Don't just hope for a brighter future or more income, be realistic. Many of the families hurt by the real estate bubble could have seen for themselves the trouble they were in had they simply prepared a basic budget and then compared their income with their expenses together with their prospective mortgage payment. You must look at your mortgage payment in advance to see if it fits into your budget, considering all of your monthly expenses, car payment(s) and other bills, the works. Don't put your head in the sand and hope. Be proactive and never take on a mortgage you can't comfortably afford.

2. **Borrow one step beneath your ability.**

Try and make every decision regarding the amount you will borrow and the home you will buy one step under what you can actually afford. You will thank me later. Remember, you have to earn enough money to make those mortgage payments each month. In a sense, you are setting up your work responsibilities for the next 15 to 30 years, so don't put too many hours on your schedule.

3. **Fixed at all cost.**

There are many types of loans, but the universal loan of choice would have to be the one on which you can rely upon as always bearing the same rate, a fixed rate.

4. **Wait for the rate.**

If you can't get the rate and costs you want or can afford for your purchase or refinance, then wait for them. There is never a rush to make a bad financial decision and, trust me; there will always be another home, another car, another loan, etc. Most salespeople rush you at just the moment that you should not be rushed. The salesperson or mortgage broker is not going to be making your mortgage payments, you are. "I am sending you out like sheep among wolves. Therefore be as shrewd as snakes and as innocent as doves." Matthew 10:16 NIV

5. **Don't have seconds.**

Do not take out a second mortgage. A first mortgage is already a 30 year commitment, so why would you add a second. If you have a second mortgage, work hard toward knocking it out before making any other purchases. A home equity line can be good for an emergency; but, remember, a home equity line is basically a second mortgage with a checkbook attached to it. It is a lien against your home; and if things go south, you may loose your home. If the only way you can buy a home is by taking out a second mortgage, then save your money.

6. **Lose 10 years in 10 seconds.**

Well it is not quite 10 seconds, but that might be the time it takes to write an extra check for $150 or so each month toward your first mortgage payment. If you add an extra $150 a month towards principal on a $100,000 mortgage at 6% interest, you will knock about 10 years off the loan. Ten years! Imagine what 10 years less of mortgage payments could mean for your financial future? Imagine paying off your house at 35 instead of 45; 45 instead of 55 and so on. Mark your extra check "principal payment", drop it in the mail each month, and you may be—that quickly—able to turn your 30 year mortgage into a 20 year mortgage. A little extra each month can go a long way toward shortening your loan term. Think that wouldn't make a difference in your financial future? It will and big time!

7. **Pay it off**.

Part of being financially independent is paying off your home. I remember at the beginning of the real estate crisis speaking with a realtor on a trip back from Vail, Colorado. I asked if home prices were dropping in high end resort areas, like Beaver Creak, Vail and Aspen, as I would have figured they would have. The reply shocked me as the realtor related that most owners and buyers there were cash buyers and therefore had no mortgage to worry about and so the crisis had not really affected them yet. The wealthy have paid off their homes and they can survive the high times and the low times. Try and stay in your first home as long as possible and pay it off. If you can make that happen, you will reap the benefits for years. Imagine the incredible flexibility and financial ability you would have if your home were paid off. It is long term planning, but starting early can save you years and years of mortgage payments. Remember, each time you move you may be restarting the 30 year clock. Even thirty years is just too long to wait, so plan to shorten your payoff clock with extra payments, and plant yourself until you've paid it off. That's certainly one method toward financial freedom and independence.

8. **Interest only is phony baloney**.

Paying interest only is the road to nowhere. It's like only taking enough money to the amusement park to pay the parking fee. You go through the all the aggravation of getting there, paying the parking fee and then get stopped at the gate, with no chance to enjoy the rides. If you can only afford a loan "interest only", you're in trouble and you can't afford the loan. Are you already in an "interest only" loan? If you are, get an extra job, cut expenses, refinance, do something to start knocking down the balance.

9. **Get two good faith estimates.**

Your lender or mortgage broker will need to give you a good faith estimate soon after your loan application. The good faith estimate tells you how many points you will be charged, preferably one or less. It also tells you what your loan fees will be, escrows, closing costs, interest rate and the approximate monthly payment. You will want to get two good faith estimates to compare costs, points and loan fees from two different lenders. This is the best way to help you spot if you are being wildly overcharged. Rates and points are driven in part by your credit, and how you are viewed and treated from lender to lender can vary. You may also want to have your good faith estimate reviewed by your accountant or real estate attorney because a thirty minute review can save you the aggravation and cost of going through with a bad loan. Remember this is the beginning of your loan process and you must be careful and make a wise decision.

10. **Put 20% down and avoid MIP.**

Do you think the bank's doing you a favor by letting you buy with no money down? Think again. The higher the risk for the bank, the higher the costs and charges will be for you. If you can wait to buy your home until you have 20% to put down, you will be ahead of the game and you will be starting off right. Now everyone can't do this, but it's worth the wait and it achieves a number of things at once. With 20% down you will avoid MIP which stands for Mortgage Insurance Premium. This is a monthly fee you will pay to insure the lender against your own default. MIP is of no benefit to you and it is generally lost money. Part of the problem with the recent mortgage meltdown is that so many people bought homes with no money down that there was no equity to survive the downturn and no equity to facilitate a refinance. "But the bank says they can give me an 80/20 loan to avoid MIP and that I'll be able to buy with no money down." An 80/20 loan tries to compensate for your inability to put 20% down by finding another bank or investor to put it down for you. It avoids MIP, which can be expensive, but it doesn't come without cost. The 20% second mortgage holder will generally charge you a higher rate of interest, and you'll have no equity at all. Two payments for the price of one home!

Second Mortgages and Home Equity Lines

Taking out a second mortgage or home equity line is literally the mortgaging and pledging of one's future and one's children's inheritance. Do you know the meaning and origin of the word "mortgage"? It derives from the Latin terms "mort" meaning "death" and "gage" meaning "pledge"; i.e. "Death Pledge". It was a pledge of property with the idea that the debt would be repaid in full upon death. These types of additional loans put you in jeopardy of default and so they should not be taken lightly. Your home's equity is your future and your children's inheritance. I've heard many people say, "I'm spending my children's inheritance." Well, God refers to us as his heirs and children, and he has designated the land of Israel as an inheritance for his chosen people.

> Now if we are children, then we are heirs—heirs of God and co-heirs with Christ, if indeed we share in his sufferings in order that we may also share in his glory.
>
> Romans 8:17 NIV

There is an inheritance for us from the Lord and, as good stewards; we should seek to leave one for our children. Equity in one's home facilitates future refinances, lower rates, and the option to sell one's home in a pinch. The modern real estate bubble with all the second mortgages, 80/20 loans and the like have sucked out all the equity from our homes and placed debtors in more debt bondage than has ever been known. If you don't have a second mortgage or home equity loan, don't take one out. Remember, your home is your safest and most important asset unless you sign it away in the form of a mortgage or home equity loan.

CHAPTER 6

Student Loans

"The Ostrich Effect"

We know that an education is both good and important. The twelve disciples had about a three year graduate education from the ultimate source of wisdom and knowledge. Their benefactor of insightful understanding was referred to in the scriptures as "Rabboni" or master. He taught as one with authority. When defending himself against his detractors and justifying his position and knowledge, he made one of the most profound statements ever made, "before Abraham was born, I am!" John 8:58 NIV. He is and was, of course, Jesus. His teachings were always in the form of parables, illustrative stories, and we can learn a great deal from them. The disciples, however, were not in astronomical debt after their studies under Jesus.

Post graduate education is an important aspect of our lives. A college degree is required for many jobs; and with each additional degree, your earning potential can increase dramatically. Yet it is not without cost. Many of today's students graduate with loans the size of mortgages. They are almost never dischargeable in bankruptcy and so you are going to have to plan on paying back every cent, so put it in your budget. If you can avoid taking out a student loan, do so at all cost; work an extra job, take it a little slower, or choose a lower cost school. It's critical that you carefully evaluate how much you are going to borrow; if there is any way to borrow less, borrow less.

It's amazing how many people incur student loan after student loan only to continue to defer payment on them. They become so large that it's like walking around with the Hindenburg on a string and pretending that there's nothing wrong. The problem is that student loans don't go away and they certainly don't fade away. Student loans are also generally not dischargeable in a bankruptcy for obvious reasons and failure to pay on them can result in your wages being garnished. With all this in play, I still continue to meet so many that have what I call "The Ostrich Effect" toward their student loan debt. They put their head in the sand and pretend they don't see it, putting it off and putting it off. Deferral is a wonderful thing, in moderation. During school, income is low and it's not a practical moment to pay down the debt. However, once you graduate, constant deferrals and even worse, additional student loans only increase a must-solve problem.

So what do you do? Well if you want to be debt free, you're going to have to face your debt head on, place your student loans into your budget and get started. Start with a ten year repayment plan. The key is to start. Paying off my student loans took what seemed like an eternity. But now, it seems like an eternity ago. Many student loans bear a low interest rate and their payment may also be low. Whatever the case may be, they will not go away on their own, and you will need to knock them out. Get started! Whatever you do, don't borrow more money just to defer their payment, as more debt is just increasing and lengthening your pain. Start paying on them, keeping track of their balances on a monthly basis, and before you know it, they will be gone. If you can, add extra money each month to your payment and you may be able to cut down the payoff time in half.

What if you're still incurring more student loan debt and you're in school? Well education is critical in this modern world in terms of future income and qualifications; however, remember that every cent you borrow you will have to pay back. Be frugal with your borrowed loan; try and keep it to a minimum. If you can work a side job to reduce what you borrow or live with parents instead of on campus, that's all the better. Also, never use student loans for your normal living expenses. Why? First, the purpose of a student loan is to pay for tuition and, in some cases, room and board; however, you're incurring a debt which is set off by an asset, your education. Living expenses are a normal expense that you should be working to meet each month. When you start borrowing student loan funds to pay living expenses, you're deficit spending big time, not building an asset. You don't want to be paying for groceries, a watch, and a room that you had ten years ago.

Cosigning a Student Loan

Never cosign anything! Is that clear enough for you? I could go down a long list of clients that were being garnished or harassed for their adult child's student loan which they unwittingly cosigned. For the most part, you're much better contributing toward your son or daughter's education directly then cosigning their loans. Give them the money, pay for their books, mail a check to the tuition office, but don't cosign. Remember, this is a book for those in financial trouble. If you have plenty of money, put your children a step ahead by keeping them out of debt. But, if your not doing well yourself or just barely making your bills, you don't need an additional loan obligation which you may never be able to get rid of without paying it off. Do you know how many parents are being garnished for their adult son or adult daughter's defaulted student loan because they cosigned for it? Typically, if a bank refuses to make a loan without a cosigner, it's because they have determined that the prospective borrower is a high risk for default. Federal student loans, however, already have one guarantor or at least insurer, the government. This generally allows a student, without much credit, to get such a loan. That is also why they are not dischargeable in bankruptcy, as the government is the insurer; and the government has no interest in facilitating their own discharge. If you cosign a loan, you are a guarantor on the loan. When you cosign, you're guaranteeing the lender that the moment your very reliable son, daughter or friend fails to write a check, you will write that check in their stead. It's not fiction; it's a fact that there are many, many parents, friends and relatives who are paying for defaulted loans on which they cosigned. This is, of course, in addition to their debts. You would be better off simply paying your child's tuition or paying their debt outright then cosigning for it. In any case, if you co-sign, make sure you have your checkbook in hand and that your budget has a provision for the potential, and in many cases, likely default.

9 GUIDING RULES FOR STUDENT LOANS

1. **Keep your head out of the sand.**

Start paying back your student loans early and avoid endless deferrals. Track your balances each month and you'll knock them out sooner than you think. If you ignore them, they won't ignore you. Putting your head in the sand will just result in your future wages being garnished.

2. **Budget your payment.**

Get your student loan onto your budget and aggressively pay off your student loan. At worst, set it up for a ten year repay and see if you can add more each month to shorten the payoff to five years and so on. Remember, the key is to start.

3. Never co-sign a student loan.

If you sign it, you've bought it. Help your children directly by paying for their books and providing them room and board at home. If you want to help them with school, mail in a payment or pay some tuition. Remember, if you co-sign, plan on paying for a four year college education, minus the diploma.

4. Minimize your exposure.

Don't keep taking out loans just to defer your payment. Loans are like taxes in that the only way to get rid of them is to pay them off. Start the clock early on paying them back and only borrow what you need for tuition.

5. Community College

If you are not rolling in the dough, a community college for the first two years can save you thousands in debt while still providing you with a great education.

6. Don't borrow room and board.

It's great to go away to school, but if you can avoid adding the equivalent of a new car loan to your student loan bill, you will have a much easier future. You can still have a great college experience while living at home.

7. Deferral can put you in peril.

Simply deferring your student loan does nothing for you and simply puts off the battle to eliminate your debt. Attack. Attack. Attack.

8. I'm already being garnished, now what?

A student loan garnishment may be a blessing in disguise because you have to pay the bill anyway. Monitor your balance each month to ensure your debt is decreasing. If the garnishment is beyond your ability, contact the lender to see if you can work out a lower payment or an attorney if it's too overwhelming. If you are being garnished for your child's school bill, it's time for a serious one on one with junior on financial responsibility; i.e., they need to contact the lender to make a payment arrangement.

9. No New Debt

With giant student loans, you are in no position to be incurring any new debt. You do not need luxury items, no new credit cards, no new cars. Knock out the student loans first and add the extra funds you would have spent on the luxuries of life to eliminate your debt.

CHAPTER 7

Car Loans

Serious Business, Serious Consequences

> A repossessed car, whether or not voluntary, is financially disastrous and can put you into a bankruptcy.
> Steven Cohen, Esq.

If it sounds like overkill, it's not! Car loans are serious business, and the dealership that sold you that car so aggressively is generally also an aggressive collector. I would even venture to say that car loans are the most viciously collected debts out there. If your car is repossessed or voluntarily returned to the dealer, it will likely be sold at private auction for far less than what is owed, with the resulting deficiency brought against you in the form of a lawsuit. Attempted garnishment of income and assets will likely follow. Well, what does all that mean? It means don't bite off more than you can chew. Many families are tipped over the edge into crisis by that car that looked too good to pass up, too awesome to leave behind at the dealer. Many also knew the moment they made the purchase that they had no business taking on a $600 monthly car payment. If you are having financial problems or have a lot of credit card debt, you have no business buying a new car and certainly no business incurring a high car payment. Regardless of income, the more you get into debt, the more likely you are to default. Don't ignore the risk, take it to heart and you will be well served.

Here is what I have seen over the years in terms of car payments and their relationship to default. I have divided them into four levels and my take on each level of payment. Obviously, individual incomes and debt tolerances will vary, but you'll get the idea with the four levels of car payments that are laid out below. After dealing with hundreds of families in trouble, car payments have come to be somewhat of a barometer of their situation.

Car Payments: 4 Levels into Trouble

$299 and less

This is where you should be if you have over $5,000 in credit card debt. One of the key problems that debtors have in trying to catch up on debt is their complete inability to reduce an overwhelming car payment. So don't start with one and it will not bring you down.

$300 to $450

These are middle of the road, normal car payments. One car payment can be handled gingerly. Two can topple you if you are also carrying a good amount of credit card debt.

$500 to $650

Now you're pushing the envelope because a higher car payment reduces your ability to pay other debts down and gives you little leeway in times of trouble. If you have financial problems there is no doubt why if you have an over $500 a month car payment. This amount combined with another car payment or credit card debt will strain any budget.

$700 to $1000

This is the ozone layer for car payments and for big trouble. Sign up for this type of payment and it's a wonder if the salesperson can keep a straight face. You have to know that nothing good can happen with a car payment which is equivalent to many people's rent. Don't do it unless you can say that you're flowing with money; and, if you are, buy the car for cash.

Well, we all need a car and so what should you do the next time you are in the market for a vehicle. Universally, I have found two common factors for virtually all the individuals I have met in a debt crisis.

The first factor is a lack of planning. The second factor is the absence of a budget. So with that in mind, you are going to plan in advance and budget in advance for your next car purchase. Planning means taking the time to research your prospective car purchase before you step foot out your door. To budget your car purchase means to work out on paper how much you can comfortably afford taking into account your other bills. Remember, before you scoff at the idea of a budget, a car purchase is the 2nd largest purchase you will likely make in your lifetime. With the real estate markets decline, some cars are of an equivalent cost to many condos and even some small homes. So it's a big deal and a car loan is typically a five to six year commitment. Take it seriously and err on the side of caution. You'll notice I used the terms "comfortably afford" when I discussed your budgeting for the purchase. The goal of this text is to keep you out of trouble not to get you into it. If you buy one step or level under what you can afford you'll thank me during tougher times. If you underspend, you can bank the difference. If you overspend, have fun working a second job and worse yet, stressing at night over how to make the payment. Remember, you are in charge of your own budget and not the car salesperson. He or she will not be making the monthly payment and just because they can get you out the door with the vehicle does not mean you should buy it. Here are two questions for you: First, do your grandparents have a high car payment? Second, are they wise or foolish? Well, I hope you'll say they are wise and that their car was either paid off years ago or that they drive an economical vehicle. Keep that in mind when your shopping. So with all this in mind, here are my top ten rules when buying a car:

MY TOP 10 RULES FOR CAR PURCHASES

1. Online Pricing First

You will never out negotiate a car dealer and that advice comes straight from an attorney, so don't try. Use an online service to find the vehicle's invoice price and what the car you want should sell for. Some online services and memberships will actually do the negotiating for you; and, with this in hand, you should achieve the best pricing. If not, go to the next dealer. Never be afraid to walk out and keep looking; that's part of getting the best price.

2. Check your budget.

Don't go to the dealer before you have determined what payment you can actually afford. Remember, go one step below what you can afford, not to your limit. If you have a lot of debt already, don't buy a car; use what you have.

3. One Vehicle Per Income

One vehicle payment per income means that if your spouse is not working, you should only have one car payment. Never have more than two car or vehicle payments at once. This includes boats, motorcycles and the like.

4. Don't break the sound barrier.

If you have more than $5,000 of credit card debt, your payment should be under $400 a month. However, under no circumstance should you break the payment sound barrier which we will loosely call $600 a month.

5. Economy pays.

You can save an extra $50-$100 a month simply by picking a fuel efficient car. The difference between the fuel efficiency of 25 mpg car and a 30 mpg car is about 20%, and that's considerable. You can take the better fuel efficiency and laugh all the way to the bank.

6. At all costs, don't default.

"I can't afford it, now what?" Well don't default or hand it back in. You'll be demolished financially. Trade it in, sell it and pay the difference or borrow from somewhere else. Do anything you can to avoid default. Default creates more debt than you can imagine, with nothing in return; and it's the quickest road traveled to bankruptcy.

7. Don't accept a crazy interest rate.

Do you know that every car purchase has at least two stages of negotiation? You may win the price war on the car and be destroyed on the loan without even realizing it. Car loans and the flexibility that dealers have in pricing them for you are incredibly broad. I was once informed at a dealership upstairs that my credit was so good it would help their credit rating; and downstairs—when I was filling out the forms for the loan—I was informed that my credit was just "so so". What changed? It wasn't my credit; it was the profit that could be made on giving me a higher interest rate loan. I informed the loan officer of his oversight and then received a smile and a better loan. If you can't get a sensible interest rate at the dealer, then don't buy the car. What is sensible is going to vary from time to time. However, if you take a good borrower as getting around 6%, then don't get a loan at 12% or more. A crazy interest rate is simply the way to disaster regardless of the payment amount. If all you can qualify for is a loan with a rate of 15% or more, take the bus or carpool until you are back on your feet. An awful looking clunker is better than a crazy interest rate car loan. You can't be spending twice as much as others and hope to get ahead. A general guideline would be 9% as the limit for a car loan interest rate; failing which buy a cheap used car and start building your savings and your credit. Be willing to negotiate and walk out and you will be surprised at how much leeway the dealer suddenly has. Stand fast and leave. The only way you can know your own true limit is if you walk out on two dealers. It may sound crazy, but you're the one who has to pay the debt back. Then you'll know you have called their bluff. Remember, the higher the rate the higher the risk. This principle applies to them and to you; and if the rate and risk are too high, you shouldn't be buying the car.

8. Used Cars

The sad thing about buying a used car is that sometimes used car dealerships are pricing them at or close to the price of a new car and saddling the buyer with a high loan to boot. They are also frequently pricing them far higher then the true value and what they paid. You must check the value online before you buy. Be sure to get an online history report first. Used car buying is dangerous business in the sense of the unknown. How many cars have you traded in and said, "That next buyer is getting a perfectly well-oiled machine that runs great with no worries." Baloney! You're much better off buying the cheapest new car on the market than buying a used car at a high price. If you are buying used, get it looked over by a mechanic and buy for cash. Then you will at least have avoided the debt. Even if you buy a cheap clunker, you may have at least avoided a high car payment. If you're in a financial bind, think of it as a temp car until you get back on your feet. You can always spend more later, but you can never go back and spend less.

9. Try your bank first.

Before you go to the dealer, see if your own bank will approve you for a car loan; find out the amount you can borrow and determine the rate. This can help you immensely in setting up your own financing in a low pressure environment and will probably yield a lower rate with better terms.

10. Don't buy on emotion.

You can't allow yourself to make a disastrous financial decision based on emotion. Know what you want and what you want to pay before you go shopping for a car. Do not allow yourself to be talked into a more expensive car because the dealer can get the payments within your range or just simply because you're approved. Your approval by the dealer for the loan does not guarantee your ability to make the payments on the car. Remember you're the one that is promising to make those 60 payments, and 60 payments can seem like a lifetime if the payments are high.

CHAPTER 8

Discretionary Purchases

A man once asked Jesus if he could follow along with him, maybe with the hopes of cashing in on what seemed to be a profitable venture with a supernatural healer who drew great crowds with a new message. The reply given was surprising and demonstrated what our Lord's focus was really on, and it was not on material concerns.

> Jesus replied, "Foxes have dens and birds have nests, but the Son of Man has no place to lay his head."
>
> Matthew 8:20 NIV

Not the kind of sales pitch you give to those seeking to cash in. When you feel convinced that you cannot live without some new purchase, a new car, some furniture or some clothing, consider that the Lord had nothing and he lived a very sacrificial life. Surprisingly, however, I have yet to meet someone that was pushed over the financial edge with frivolous furniture purchases. You see, at least with furniture, you have something tangible and something that will last for many years to come. Quite the opposite is true with aimless credit card purchases. I have many times seen individuals with $50,000 to $100,000 of credit card debt and less than $1000 of personal property to show for it. It may seem impossible but just consider the carrying costs of $100,000 in credit card debt at 29% interest. Well that's $29,000 a year in interest alone and that's before you take into account compounded interest, late fees, etc. You're not going to pay back that kind of debt without a phenomenal income and a miracle or two. The important factor with any expenditure is to get value for your purchase and to have a plan to pay it off.

Zero Percent Interest

Talk about bait and switch, if you don't pay off a zero percent offer within the time period allowed be prepared for the switch. If you are buying furniture, you can many times get a zero percent interest loan for the first year, but do plan to pay it off within that year. If you don't, the lender will typically add all the accumulated interest and you will suddenly be paying 18% to 29% more than your original purchase price. What? But I thought I got such a good deal, zero percent! I wasn't paying attention to the payoff date! That's what the lender is counting on. You see, the most profitable consumer to the credit companies is the one who buys on emotion, with no plan for payoff and no concern about what they are being charged. This is also the case with credit cards that offer short term 0% interest advances. The idea is to bait you, like a fish, into taking the loan. You are put at ease as to the cost and your lack of funds because it's an interest free loan or a purchase with deferred payments. The only problem is that it's really only interest free for a short period and if you don't have a plan to pay it off on time, you are going to pay through the nose after the initial period. Saying, "We'll pay it off in a year" is meaningless talk unless you have a plan. Saying, "We'll pay it off in a year because our budget has an extra $300 a month which we can apply to the furniture" is a plan and a good one at that.

5 RULES FOR DISCRETIONARY PURCHASES

1. Have a payoff plan.

If you're buying interest free for a year, pay it off in a year. Don't wait a year to figure out what you can pay. When you sign your name on the purchase order, you should already have said to your spouse, "We will pay $200 a month for 10 months and it will be paid off."

2. Start paying now.

Zero percent (0%) interest for a year does not mean wait 364 days and then start making payments. That attitude is for the uninformed. The Bible relates that:

> For whoever has will be given more, and they will have an abundance. Whoever does not have, even what they have will be taken from them.
>
> Matthew 25:29 NIV

If you don't pay off a 0% interest rate loan in a year, then you didn't get a 0% interest loan, you got a 29% interest loan and another high interest rate debt to pay off. Imagine getting a great set of furniture at 10% off and then having 29% interest added to your bill. That's what will happen if you don't plan to pay off your "No Interest" loan. You see, the creditor that loaned the money for the furniture has quite a surprise for you if you go one minute over the deadline date. It's typically called 18% to 29% interest, and interest is typically accruing from the day you make the purchase. They are dreaming at night about you missing the payoff date or being too busy taking care of other matters.

3. Never, Never, Never let yourself pass the 0% interest rate period.

Don't turn the lender's dream of adding back accrued interest into reality. If you do, the 0% dream interest deal you received may vanish and be replaced by a 29% nightmare.

4. Have a budget for your purchase in advance.

If you're barely making it each month, then you're not in a position to make a purchase. Look at your budget in advance. If you're keeping a monthly budget, you will know exactly how much extra you have each month. You need to have an idea in advance so that you don't go in with a $3600 budget and come out with $8600 of purchases.

5. Don't ignore reality.

Be realistic. If you cannot afford the purchase or if you are already in debt, don't even look.

CHAPTER 9

Dead Weight Debt

It's time for a crash debt diet!

All debts outside of one home mortgage and one car loan are dead weight debts. Sounds too simple? Well, typically those looking at bankruptcy or who are facing a financial crisis, have a myriad of debts such as multiple car loans, first and second mortgages, multiple credit cards and the like. A great part of our population is not only overweight in pounds from overeating junk food; they are also overweight in debt, out of control debt. You know that extra weight you've been meaning to loose for all those years? Think of all the health problems associated with being overweight. It's so bad that many health insurance providers actually exclude coverage for "morbid obesity." I know mine does. "Morbid Obesity"—that sounds terrible! It must be more common than you think if you have to receive notices from the insurance company alerting customers that they don't cover it. Think for a second what the term means: "Morbid" meaning death or leading to death and "Obesity" meaning grossly overweight.

Are you morbidly obese in debt? Are you carrying so much debt that you're approaching financial death? Sounds awful but that's what "dead weight debt" does to you. It leads you nowhere good; and carrying a lot of it is simply a time bomb leading to the point of disaster. Are you carrying debt weight debt? Can you look into the future and see where 15, 20 or 30k of credit card debt is leading you? Being overweight in debt <u>will</u> have, not might have, a deadly result on your future finances. That's why you have to take action now, not when you're so far gone and so overweight in debt that there's no other option than bankruptcy. Now bankruptcy can be a wonderful solution to a seemingly unsolvable problem and can many times offer a "fresh start" to those over the edge. However, the aim of this book is to put you on a self-made course for a healthy financial future. A self started debt diet.

No one thinks they're overweight in pounds or debt until they take a truly good look in the mirror. I know from personal experience that being thirty pounds overweight caused me higher blood pressure, migraine headaches and additional stress from having high blood pressure not to mention the frequent doctor visits to see what was wrong with me. It took me a trip to the hospital for kidney stones and being told my blood pressure was a little high to shock me into action. You see, before the hospital trip, I was blinded by the world as to the true effects of eating poorly. Whatever I wanted I ate: milkshakes, donuts, soda, salty foods, and so on. I wasn't fat, but I wasn't eating healthy either. Fast food stops don't weigh you and ask you to get out of line; they say, "May I take your order please?" Wild overeating is like saying, "Yes, I'll have a heart attack, high blood pressure, high cholesterol, a shorter lifespan and a myriad of heath issues." Well, if you overspend and spend out of control, you're saying the same thing each time you use your credit card; "I'll have a delayed retirement, possible bankruptcy, harassing creditor calls, arguments with my husband or wife and a ten year struggle until I figure it out." For myself, health wise after the hospital visit, I realized I didn't want to be stuck on medication and have health problems for the rest of my life. To do this, I knew I was going to have to make a radical change. That change couldn't be minimal; it had to be deliberate and direct. I cut out unhealthy foods from my diet, started an exercise program and looked for ways to control previous impulsive behaviors. Well, it didn't take long to see the effect—better health, no more migraines, etc. The same principle applies to debt. Take immediate steps to stop the spending, concentrate on reducing debt and begin a savings program. You will soon see results and usually dramatic ones.

You can change your ways! You can cut out the fat, the spending fat that's slowly killing you financially! Don't wait until you are so financially sick that you feel beyond recovery. If you're already debt heavy, it's time for a crash debt diet to start you on the way back to financial fitness.

So what are these dead weight debts and what can you do about them? Dead weight debts are extra debts which you're just not designed to maintain financially. They are the result of making deficit purchases on credit, far beyond your current ability to afford. You must knock them out! If you want a luxury item, buy it for cash, not on credit. What good is it to buy something on sale and save 10%, if you're putting it on a card that's going to charge you 25% interest?

CHAPTER 10

Credit Cards

The King of Dead Weight Debts

Which king do you serve? The King of Kings or the King of Dead Weight Debts? To whom is your allegiance? To whom do you pay the most tribute? This question is not meant to challenge your faith, as there are many fine Christians with tremendous debt. No, it is meant to help you focus on the true and devastating cost which credit cards can bear. Credit cards are both powerful and lethal. They allow one to wield incredible power. With a credit card you can be on a cruise to Alaska in a week, a plane to Paris in a day and can spend a fortune on clothes and jewelry in just a matter of hours. Yet the consequences are grave. High rates reign in credit card debt. How much do you think the loan shark on the corner charges for his money? Is it really that much more than the 29% you could possibly be paying your credit card company? Scary to think that intelligent beings, me included, can be lulled into thinking that making a purchase on a 29% credit card is okay or normal. What if your brother offered to loan you $1000 at 29%, 18% or even 13% interest? Would you question his faith? You would likely be outraged and completely insulted. You might even call him a thief and a robber to offer you such terms. If that's the case, why would you ever consider making such purchases on credit cards? Well, the answer is more complex than it seems. We are lulled into thinking our rates are low by introductory offer after introductory offer. Those offering us such rates really want to build a sense of complacency so we are relatively unaware when the higher rates kick in. This is further buttressed by the minimally low payments that are required to maintain such debts.

Understanding the Credit Card Trap

> Be alert and of sober mind. Your enemy the devil prowls around like a roaring lion looking for someone to devour.
>
> 1 PETER 5:8 NIV

In a world where you have a seemingly free will to choose between right and wrong, you also have a seemingly inexhaustible set of choices when it comes to your spending. America is a land of freedom, but with freedom comes responsibility. Unfortunately, we are encouraged by the world we live in to have anything we want, whenever we want. What ever happened to thinking like our grandparents, who would save for months and even years before making a purchase? Now we are offered instant credit at every turn. Thousands can be spent in a matter of moments. With all this freedom has come an idea that borrowing to make purchases is good and normal. It has been taken one step further with the convenience of the credit card. The credit card has given families the ability to sell their future labor by borrowing money to make purchases today. There is a very loose connection, if any at all, between the credit we are granted and our actual ability to pay debt back. Add to it companies that do nothing but encourage you to borrow and spend, craftily inviting you into a harrowing atmosphere replete with financial danger. Over the years I have seen so many people far over their heads in debt. The disparity between what they could truly afford and what their credit lines were was truly amazing. It was equally as amazing to see so many very smart individuals, myself included, making the catastrophically bad decision of making purchases on credit.

    Credit cards have truly become a modern day adversary of epic proportion.
You can't possibly hope to defeat such an adversary without first understanding where they come from and what they are doing. Do you think your credit cards are at your disposal? Do you think that credit cards are there to serve you? Do you think that credit cards are just a harmless tool to bridge the gap between what you want and what you can afford? Be sober, be vigilant, because your credit cards are not your friends; they are very expensive lending tools offered to you at extremely high rates of interest which yield tremendous profits for the corporations that operate them. They can also have devastating financial effects on the unwitting consumer

who is drawn into the credit card trap. The trap is set through the complacency of the consumer who does not realize the ingenious financial forces they are dealing with and the cunning and well though out plans and fees in place at every turn. Credit cards have a vicious and voracious appetite for your money, and they are seeking whom they may devour with fees and high rates of interest. Credit card companies snare the unsuspecting consumer into a seemingly inescapable trap which slowly tightens over time.

If you were at a circus, you might see and even be willing to hold a Boa constrictor. The Boa constrictor is a slow moving snake which can seems quite harmless and which many have enjoyed holding in their arms. Yet the Boa defeats its prey through stealth and by slowly and seemingly harmlessly moving into position around their prey. Slowly they curl around their target in an almost loving embrace. But the embrace is not love, it is a tightening constriction which cannot be escaped from and is usually discovered only after it is too late. This is what happens, more often then not, with so many fine Christians and non-Christians alike. They are lulled into a sense of complacency, borrowing more and more over time while the interest rates increase and their payments stay relatively low. As time moves on, they are encouraged to borrow more and more, with cash advances and check offers claiming to offer low introductory rates and a "pay it off later" mentality. However, after a period of time the rates and balances start to squeeze the consumer to an almost inescapable point. The debtor is offered little solace by the creditor who simply informs him at his moment of need that he signed the creditor's agreement and the charges are in accordance with his card's agreement.

Have you ever truly examined your monthly billing statement? Have you seriously considered the devastating effect of a late payment? Do you know that a $39 late payment on a $390 balance is a return for the credit card company of an extra 10%, just for that month? If you were late each month for a year, you would be paying an extra 120% interest in addition to your normal rate. Have you read your most recent "change in terms" disclosure? Did it reduce your rate or change the terms to your benefit? Although there have been some recent legislated improvements in credit terms and charges to the consumer, generally changes are not to your benefit. You've heard the saying, "Read it and weep!" The term is frequently applied to gambling, specifically to the loser whose cards expose the truth that he or she has lost their money to their opponent. Well, it's not much different when it comes to credit card terms. They are written with the most cunning foresight into removing the money from your wallet and placing it into the coffers of your creditors. It is legal but not to your benefit. They are designed to charge the unwitting card member for each and every misstep in cascading effect. Perhaps reading this little rhyme will help you be dealt a better hand in the future:

> ## "A credit rhyme that will save your dime"
>
> Miss a payment and you're late,
> add a late charge, up the rate.
> It's great business for the card,
> but the penalty will hit you hard.
> Keep on spending, you'll be broke;
> get out now before you choke.
> Quick, a budget is the key;
> lower your rates and you'll see,
> there is hope, there is light,
> if your budget plans it right.
> So pen to paper and you'll see,
> you really can become debt free!
>
> Steven Cohen, Esq.

Not every credit card company deals with the consumer with cold-hearted calculation. There are some caring companies which will forgive late charges and will work with consumers. However, once you realize that your company has no mercy and no interest in ever waiving fees or lowering rates, get out quickly. Whatever the case may be, you have to budget to become debt free.

Living on Credit Cards is for the Dogs

Living on and incurring high credit card debt is like living your financial life in "Doggy Years." What does that mean? Well, credit card debt is so severely lopsided in cost to the consumer that, if you were to compare normal loans to credit card loans, there is no comparison. It's like comparing human years to doggy years. Meaning, $5000 in credit card debt is like $15,000 in regular debt because credit cards generally carry three to four times the normal rate of interest. Think about the concept. Compare owing $20,000 on a car loan to owing $20,000 in credit card debt. There is no comparison. Twenty thousand owed on a car at 6% is not so bad, maybe $400 or so a month over 5 years. But owe $20,000 on a credit card at 24% interest and you may be on the brink of bankruptcy, and the $400 a month you're paying will just cover interest into perpetuity. Need a further example? Let's look at the same scenario again: Car loan of $20,000 at 6% and Credit Card(s) for $20,000 at 24%. The car loan interest starts at $100 per month. The credit card interest starts at $400 per month. That's 300% more a month in interest. Now do you see the doggy year's comparison? It will take you three times as long to pay off your indebtedness because the rate is three times as much. The exact same amount of money is owed, but the car loan is 5 yeas and the credit card loan is 15 to 20 years! Well, you know the rest of the story. Virtually no one can take a 300% hit each month and still be viable. Thus, the problem is exposed. There is really no way to win with credit cards if you carry a high balance! If you carry a balance, the higher the balance the more devastating the effect and the more severe the consequences will be. Next time you see an ad to borrow $8,000 on your card and "pay it off later", remember that "later" may be 15 to 20 years to never!

Do you work for Laban?

The quickest path to nowhere land financially is to make payments on a debt that's never paid off. Do you Remember Laban from the book of Genesis? He kept changing the rules of the game for Jacob. He was a trickster and a cheat. Jacob himself had cheated his older twin, Esau, out of the birthright by taking advantage of his brother in a time of need, but then Jacob was introduced to the ultimate swindler, Laban. Jacob was taken advantage of and tricked twice into working seven years for the same bride. Maintain a high credit card balance and you will be working over and over again for the same purchases. Donating 10% to the church is nothing when you think that you may be already donating 24% each month to your credit card company for purchases made years ago and with no earthly or heavenly blessing to follow. Let's look at the example of how much a simple toaster can cost your family if it's not paid off. Would you pay $214.86 for a toaster?

Cost of a $25 Toaster at 24% over 10 Years:

$214.86

Year	Start	Interest	Balance
1	$25.00	$6.00	$31.00
2	$31.00	$7.44	$38.44
3	$38.44	$9.23	$47.67
4	$47.67	$11.44	$59.11
5	$59.11	$14.19	$73.29
6	$73.29	$17.59	$90.88
7	$90.88	$21.81	$112.69
8	$112.69	$27.05	$139.74
9	$139.74	$33.54	$173.27
10	$173.27	$41.59	$214.86

Would you pay $214.86 for a $25 toaster? You probably have already if you've been maintaining a long term credit card balance. "What! No, you're out of your mind!" Am I? Well, just look at the numbers above. If you bought a $25 toaster on your credit card 10 years ago and have not been paying the balance off each month, you've spent about $214.86 for that toaster. THAT'S NUTS! What's even crazier is that the credit card company made almost $190 on your silly little $25 purchase. I hope you didn't buy it on sale. If you're purchasing items on sale only to put the purchase on a credit card, then there is no sale. It must be one great toaster if you were willing to spend over two hundred dollars for it. Hey, no one ever told me that before! Of course not, they have been too busy counting your money as you try and make ends meet.

One thing is obvious and for certain. YOU WILL NEVER GET AHEAD IN LIFE IF YOU MAINTAIN A CREDIT CARD BALANCE. It's virtually impossible to pay a company triple to quadruple the going rate of interest and to get ahead financially. The problem really is that after 10 years, you bought almost 10 toasters, but you only received one. That's why you're broke. Think of it, no wonder you couldn't afford anything else. No wonder you had to pass up on the new toaster, new frying pan, or pass the offering plate empty to the person to your left, and on and on, because you were too busy paying for the first toaster you bought. Did your toaster last you 10 years? No, it broke about 2 years in. That would mean that you were paying for it 8 years after it was gone. This reality is devastating when analyzed. Think of the profit made off of your back. You pay triple the normal rate of interest, pay almost 10 times the amount of your original purchase and pay for it years after it is gone. What a business plan. What a way to keep you poor, to keep others rich and to keep you paying for items long gone—all neatly packaged into a beautiful monthly statement, completely legal, with all kinds of encouragement to spend more and keep your balance going, with no financial guidance as to what it's actually doing to you whatsoever.

The True Price of Credit

Your Financial Future

In a nutshell, the true price of credit is your financial future. Credit is costing you precious years, years that you could be helping the poor, years that you could be helping a son or daughter, years that you could be traveling the beautiful world that our Lord has made. Think you could never afford to travel to the Holy Land or Paris? Count the cost of a few silly toasters on credit cards and you would be shocked at how much of your precious money has flown out the window into oblivion. Your eyes must be opened to this truth. You must understand what is happening to you financially when you carry credit card debt. You're being short changed and it's got to stop. You see, maintaining a balance on credit card is like paying for the same purchases over and over again.

Take control and take back your money. Stop paying for a whole lot of nothing and you will have a turnaround financially that is hard to imagine in your present condition. You are deceived if you think that using credit cards for normal purchases is in any way beneficial to you. What is the benefit in buying a hair bush or a meal at 18% interest? There is none, other than convenience and that's where the trap lies. If you're not paying back everything you spend at the end of the month, your deficit spending at 10%-29% interest and that's nuts.

CHAPTER 11

Medical Bills

Large unpaid medical bills are not as common a plight as one might think. This is mostly because those who incur substantial charges generally have insurance. It is also due to the fact that most people who don't have medical insurance go without, rather than incur large medical bills. In over 15 years of practicing debt defense and bankruptcy, large medical bills were generally not the controlling factor in determining a debtor's plight; they were simply an additional symptom of a larger problem. Doctors are much more interested in healing the sick than in suing the poor. The climate amidst collectors of medical debt is not generally a vicious one, but more one of working out a plan for some type of payment. This is in stark contrast to the relentless collection on some defaulted car loans which seems to come with great speed and ferocious pursuit. Medical debts may also be more readily settled than some other forms of debt.

If you do get into substantial medical debt, try the following cure:

1. Start on some form of payment plan; and, if possible, try to ensure that no interest is accruing on the debt while you're making payments.

2. Try and settle the bill. The Bible actually encourages debtors to settle their debts on the way to court. If you can't make a large lump sum offer, make a

small lump sum offer and if it's accepted, knock it out. Remember to get it in writing.

3. Explain your situation to the creditor. With medical debt, you may have a creditor that's listening and willing to work with you.

4. If negotiation fails and you are under pressure, seek counsel from an attorney. That's never a bad idea.

CHAPTER 12

Judgments and Suits

It's time for some legal help.

Why do you dial 911 in an emergency? Is it because you're in trouble? Because there is someone out there with more knowledge and capability than you have and that is precisely what is needed for the situation at hand. If you're being sued, if you're receiving letters from an attorney or if you have a judgment against you, then you need legal help. Don't act as your own doctor or attorney. There are some situations which can seem quite minor but can have devastating effects. One example of this is a letter from your condo association's attorney regarding a small outstanding assessment. You may look at this nuisance as something you will deal with later, when you have time. However, the attorney may be looking at you as subject to a foreclosure proceeding. Ignoring an initially small $100-$300 bill in that situation could result in $1500 to $2500 of attorney's fees and the loss of your home. If you think I'm blowing things out of proportion, please know that I've seen people at risk of loosing their homes for original bills as low as $35. What happens to you if you ignore a small spot of cancer on your hand? Need I say more? Any legal correspondence received should be dealt with immediately and with serious legal evaluation. Don't wait until you're being garnished and in dire straits to seek legal help.

What is a judgment? A judgment is a legal determination that you owe a creditor a certain amount of money. Once entered in a court of law, the creditor can seek its collection from you in accordance with the laws of your State. Do you have a paid off car? The creditor may be able to take it by sheriff's sale. Do you have a job? Depending on your State's laws and your spouse's income, the creditor may be able to have your wages garnished. What is garnishment? Garnishment entitles the creditor to take part of your pay check before you do. Do you have a bank account? Ignoring a judgment or suit may mean that one day when you go to withdraw money from the bank; you discover your account is frozen.

Like a Thief in the Night

You will not see it coming. If you have a judgment against you, you will generally not be forewarned of when your money or property will be taken. It will happen like a thief in the night: You will go to get some cash out of the teller machine and it won't work. Your paycheck will come and suddenly show a deduction for a garnishment. When the garnishment comes, it will not be at an opportune time. It will happen just when you need the funds most. Once you have a judgment, the negotiation stage is over, the collection stage begins, and it's not friendly. It no longer matters what you want to do, whether you were right or wrong; it's what the creditor can legally get out of you that now matters. Now you need legal advice and you need it fast. Even one day can make a difference so don't delay. The Bible has some examples of dire urgency, most strikingly stated in the book of Revelation where the author advises the listener to not even go back into one's home but to immediately flee. This is the type of respect you need to show legal dilemmas.

Years ago, a client informed me that she had a judgment against herself and I started to raise some concerns about the urgency of her situation. The client quickly brushed off my concerns and informed me that she had nothing to lose. About three weeks later, the same client left me a desperate phone message that her account had been frozen and that she couldn't pay her rent.

Settle With Your Creditor

You are going to have to make some type of payment plan if you have a judgment against yourself. With a judgment, there is no such thing as ignoring it and moving forward financially. You must resolve it in one way or another because you are not going to be buying a home or in any secure financial position until it is resolved. Judgments are also end game financial problems, meaning that once you have a judgment or suit against you, the basic financial planning option has passed. You are now in the emergency room financially because you've been, shall we say, overeating steak and ice cream and there's no time for dieting; that option is a thing of the past.

Another important question comes into play when you are in the judgment stage. Are you financially beyond the point of no return? Case in point would be someone with a $30,000 judgment against them who only earns $20,000 a year. There has to be some evaluation as to whether there is any practical way to pay off the debt. If you're living month to month and can barely feed your family, then you're not going to be able to pay off a judgment for a repossessed car. This would be the point where other options such as bankruptcy would have to be considered and evaluated by a professional. Now you are at risk, meaning the creditor is lurking around looking to devour you financially. The judgment creditor will look to see what bank you used to use to pay them, where you work and what assets you have. They may send you legal discovery, such as interrogatories which ask you where your money is held. They may also set your deposition or testimony to be taken so they can discover your assets. All this is for their benefit. You can soon see that you're in trouble once a judgment is entered. So what do you do if your already sitting with a judgment or if you have been sued?

> **Four guiding rules if you are sued or already have a judgment against you:**

1. Consult with an attorney immediately. The time for self help has passed.
2. Don't ignore the problem, it will only get worse. Ignoring a judgment or lawsuit will only put your financial future on hold and your financial present in jeopardy.
3. Plan to get out of debt by setting up a monthly payment plan for a set period of time. It won't happen by chance; you are going to have to make a planned budget to pay off the debt in a set period of time. A simple spreadsheet can be quickly put together allowing you to actively track your balance and determine how much you can pay each month. Come up with a plan and work toward a monthly payment agreement with the creditor.
4. Determine if you are beyond the point of no return. This will allow you to consider other options such as bankruptcy which can offer you a fresh start. If you can't make a monthly payment, or the debt is so overwhelming that you feel you'll never pay it off, consult with a bankruptcy attorney.

If you are in a financial crisis, one of the most important questions you need to have answered is whether or not you are beyond the point of no return. Typically, the question I pose to debtors overwhelmed by debt is whether or not they can get out of debt on their own in three to five years. If you pose this question to yourself, and your answer is no or a complete roll of the eyes, you may want to consult with a bankruptcy attorney to evaluate your options. Debt relief was a problem even in early Biblical days. The book of Deuteronomy provided for a type of bankruptcy relief every seven years. Whether or not this period was a model for our current bankruptcy time frame is not important, what is important is that there was an understanding thousands of years ago that debt could get out of hand and that there needed to be some means for debt relief and forgiveness. The Bible carries two themes in this regard.

> But I tell you, do not swear an oath at all: either by heaven, for it is God's throne; or by the earth, for it is his footstool; or by Jerusalem, for it is the city of the Great King.
> Matthew 5:34-35 NIV

First, God knows that we are not perfect and that we are incapable of performing all our oaths. This is illustrated fairly clearly in Matthew chapter 5 where Jesus instructs us not to make oaths in the first place but just to let our yes be yes and our no be no. An oath is like a contract and to the Lord, that's serious business. If you don't make an oath, there is no risk of breaking it. The Lord actually tries to protect us from our own selves here by encouraging us not to make oaths, but to just be honorable. When you take out a large loan and sign your name guaranteeing that it will be paid back, you are in fact making an oath to the creditor that it will be paid. Do you see the danger created by your own signature? The Lord knows our failings before we do and so he encourages us not to make the oath in the first place.

> And forgive us our debts, as we also have forgiven our debtors.
> Matthew 6:12 NIV

Second, there should also be mercy as demonstrated in the Lord's Prayer. Matthew 6:12 has two parts, "forgive us our debts" and then an assuming statement "as we also have forgiven our debtors." It is asking God to forgive us and then asserting that we have also forgiven others. Therefore if we seek his forgiveness, we must also be willing to and actively forgive others. Unfortunately, there is not always the same kind of forgiveness in the real World as we would like or expect. I have many times spoken with judgment debtors who informed me that they were going to tell the judge all their problems as if the judge would then absolve the debt. Unfortunately, this is generally not the case. A judge is an enforcer of the law and will may times say, "I'm sorry, but my hands are tied, I have to follow what you contracted to do." i.e. payback the debt. It can even be reversible judicial error for a judge to use mercy as a legal basis for a ruling as opposed to following the terms of a contract. So you see how difficult it can be in our system for the debtor. Mercy is rare and we have to cherish the mercy that we are shown through our Lord Jesus in the scriptures.

CHAPTER 13

Can a Christian declare bankruptcy?

Modern families that are loosing their homes and property to creditors are nothing new. The same problems were present in Biblical times and were even endured by the Israelites. The problem became so bad that there was a year of canceling debts to protect men and women from becoming permanent slaves to their creditors.

> At the end of every seven years you must cancel debts. This is how it is to be done: Every creditor shall cancel any loan they have made to a fellow Israelite. They shall not require payment from anyone among their own people, because the LORD's time for canceling debts has been proclaimed.
> Deuteronomy 15:1-2 NIV

Imagine the careful lending that would take place if your creditor knew that they would have to cancel your debt if not repaid in 7 years?

The Bible also gives the converse example when a man with great debt who is forgiven by his creditor seeks payment for a debt from his own lesser servant. The result for the former debtor turned creditor is harsh and an admonition to all Christians, not just to seek forgiveness of debts, but to offer it in our own actions and lives.

> "Then the master called the servant in. 'You wicked servant,' he said, 'I canceled all that debt of yours because you begged me to. Shouldn't you have had mercy on your fellow servant just as I had on you?' In anger his master handed him over to the jailers to be tortured, until he should pay back all he owed.
>
> Matthew 18:32-34 NIV

It seems ironic that, under the bankruptcy code, you could file for Chapter 7 bankruptcy approximately once every seven to eight years. Was this based on the Biblical principal of Deuteronomy 15? I'll bet you never heard that question before. Whether it was or was not is not important. What is important is that the God was concerned for and understood, in both Old & New Testament days, that individuals could incur more debt than they could ever hope to pay off. In Biblical times, creditors had an even greater hand over their debtors, in that they could throw their debtors into jail until they were paid. Creditors could also have their debtors sold into slavery or ask that their relatives be sold to pay the debts. We no longer have a debtor's prison, but there are certainly numerous individuals and families out there who are feeling the wrath of their creditors.

If only the world we lived and operated under the Lord's admonition of mercy, how much more peaceful our lives would be. Sadly that is not the case and Christians and non Christians alike are hauled into court on a daily basis over debt. The stress level is so overwhelming that it is actually surprising that there are not more suicides as the options can seem fewer and farther in between. The law of this land, however, does provide an alternative to the wrath of the creditor. It is a legal alternative and a wonderful option in the midst of a disastrous financial plight. It is not a trick of law, but rather a long standing principle that those who cannot be reasonably considered to be able to pay their debts should be released from them completely, declared bankrupt and given a fresh start. It is a principle and legal provision which saves thousands of families each year from an unending cycle of vicious and unceasing debt collection. Were there not such a release valve for those unable to pay their bills, I fear we would be in a sad state where generational debt would hurt one family to the next in seeming perpetuity.

As Christians, we operate under a system of grace, not of works. You can't repay the debt you owe to God, nor can you live a perfect sinless life to earn salvation. Salvation, freedom from our indebtedness to sin, is a gift of God at no cost to you because the price was already paid through the sacrificial death and resurrection of Jesus.

For it is by grace you have been saved, through faith-and this is not from yourselves, it is the gift of God-not by works, so that no one can boast.

Ephesians 2:8-9 NIV

What is Bankruptcy anyway?

Bankruptcy is basically the legal declaration to one's creditors that the debtor is unable to pay his or her debts. There are generally two types of bankruptcies that an individual might file under, Chapter 7 and Chapter 13 of the Federal Bankruptcy code.

Chapter 7 Bankruptcy

Chapter 7 is liquidation for an individual or business, and it wipes out many types of debts to zero. Despite the term "liquidation", most debtors have few, if any, assets that will be taken by the bankruptcy Trustee. The Trustee is the individual appointed by the court to verify that you properly qualify for bankruptcy, to verify that you have been open and honest in your filing and to determine whether there are assets to administer for creditors. There are many exempt assets such as your homestead property, your retirement plans and some personal property. There are a few types of debts that are not dischargeable, such as taxes, child support, spousal support, student loans and a few intentional torts. Secured debts for things such as houses, cars and furniture which an individual wishes to keep can many times be reaffirmed, meaning there is an agreement that these items will be repaid so that the assets may be kept. If one feels that his home, car, etc., is beyond his financial means, then the asset can typically be surrendered and the debt wiped out. Many people seek bankruptcy protection in the midst of a horrible financial crisis or just when life's debts seem unsolvable in any practical period of time.

As a bankruptcy practitioner for many years, I have often said that bankruptcy is at its best, when life is at its worst! When an individual is facing lawsuits, overwhelming credit card collections, foreclosure or the like, bankruptcy is truly a release in every sense of the word. Bankruptcy can offer a solution to the seemingly unsolvable financial problems of life. It is truly a *fresh start* and that is what it is intended to be. It's like pushing the financial reset button on one's life and it can save years of struggling in a circle of disparity and debt.

Will I qualify for a Chapter 7 Bankruptcy and is it right for me? This is a question that can only be correctly answered by an experienced bankruptcy attorney who examines your situation and figures. Even with the changes to the bankruptcy code over the years, many individuals in financial distress will still qualify for bankruptcy relief. The biggest change to the bankruptcy laws of recent past was the addition of a means test which compares your income and expense with federal standards. An individual or couple with large incomes may be unable to file a Chapter 7 but still be eligible for a Chapter 13. Don't count yourself out until you have had all your figures reviewed and entered into the means test by a professional.

What about my credit? If you are looking at the bankruptcy option, your credit may already be in tatters. A bankruptcy can typically appear on your credit report for seven to ten years; however, credit can be restored over time with a good payment history so use your *fresh start* wisely. Go and spend no more! At least not on credit.

What will a Chapter 7 do for those over their heads in debt? A chapter 7 can put you on the road to recovery in months as opposed to years. If you see no other reasonable alternative than bankruptcy, the debt freedom it offers may be unrivaled.

Chapter 13 Bankruptcy

What if you are trying to save a home or simply don't qualify for a Chapter 7? We discussed briefly a Chapter 7 Bankruptcy, but there is another option for an individual or couple, Chapter 13. Chapter 13 is basically a personal reorganization and payment plan administered through a bankruptcy Trustee, a Trustee who wants you to succeed within the parameters of the law. Chapter 13 allows a debtor to place their creditors on a three to five year repayment plan with some secured creditors, such as 1st mortgage companies getting virtually all of their funds back and unsecured creditors getting a percentage of their debts paid based on a "means test" and "liquidation test" formula. A Chapter 13 can allow someone to save their home from foreclosure and to place the bank on a repayment plan. Car loans can be restructured and your financial picture remade completely. As the law is complex and the possible relief available will vary depending on your financial situation and income, you will have to first consult with an attorney to see if this is a viable option for your situation.

There is a story in the book of 2nd Kings Chapter 4 where Elisha is approached by a widow who is about to have her sons sold to creditors to pay her debts. In a miracle Elisha has her bring every jar she could find and he fills them up with oil from the Lord until there are no jars left. He then tells her the following:

> ..."Go, sell the oil and pay your debts. You and your sons can live on what is left."
> 2 Kings 4:7 NIV
>
> (Elisha to the Widow)

Bankruptcy can at times offer a great solution to very complex and seemingly impossible financial dilemma, but it will require the expertise and evaluation of an experienced attorney and should not be attempted on your own. As bankruptcy relief involves the Federal Court system, its power and protection can be great.

CHAPTER 14

Foreclosures

Who would have thought that a financial crisis reminiscent of the biblical times of Nehemiah in 444 B.C. where houses and lands were being taken could happen yet again some 2250 years later? Yet here we are again facing a crisis of epic proportion. You might think that your mortgage is a modern day invention of finance, yet not so. It was apparently alive and well in the time of Nehemiah, more than twenty- two hundred years ago. Those living in Jerusalem were losing their homes just as those in America and around the globe are loosing their homes today. God was faithful then and he will be faithful to those who serve him again today. I will deal briefly with the various options and issues which a foreclosure presents.

Time Frame

So how do you deal with a foreclosure? Well, to properly deal with a foreclosure, you are going to need to know two things from your local legal professional. First, how much time do you have to work with, weeks or months? Second, what are your realistic options? In some states the foreclosure process may move quite briskly. If you're in a State where the process can take a matter of weeks as opposed to months, your options are going to be limited and you will have to act quickly. In states like Florida where the process can easily last six months to a year or more, you will have more time to work on the situation, but even that amount of time can run out. Don't panic. Believe it or not, even though a foreclosure may seem like the end of the world, it is more likely just a giant pile of paperwork; the sole purpose of which is to legally remove you from your home so it can be sold. It may actually be a blessing in disguise if the mortgage payment was a financial nightmare for you and your family. Take heart, there will be more homes available down the road.

Realistic Options

When I say realistic options, that's what I mean. You are going to have to face reality and pursue avenues which are reachable and realistic. If your earning $35,000 a year and are trying to save or modify a loan of $250,000-$300,000, that's just not realistic. Don't waste your time on ideas that you know deep down will never work out. Your time is important and wasting Six months to a year trying to save a home which is $100,000 upside down, which you know you cannot afford anyway under any circumstance, is in most part pointless, so don't do it. Work toward realistic and achievable goals. Also, save your money aggressively while you're working on the problem. Don't stay in a home for nine months during a foreclosure, rent free, and have nothing to show for it. While you're trying to work on the problem, save your money, pay yourself rent and put it away as it will increase your options and lessen the loss. That savings may allow you to move and rent, put a down payment on another home, or even allow you to negotiate a settlement on a deficiency lawsuit.

Modifications

A modified mortgage is somewhat similar to a refinanced loan and can be simple or complex. Modifications can include a simple resumption of payments with the overdue payments placed in the rear or it may have a reduced interest rate and a partial waiver of fees and costs and even principal. Although almost everyone with the need for a modification would seek a reduction in principal, it is the least common result. For the most part, modified loans are facilitated either by a lender's in house plan or a government sponsored plan. With ever changing laws and options for borrowers in distress, you are going to have to research and vigorously pursue your options. A modified mortgage under a government sponsored plan may reduce your monthly payment and interest rate considerably for a period of years, if you qualify. Government sponsored modification plans are generally the most cost effective of options because the modification's cost to you is typically minimal and the rate reduction substantial. It is, however, an elaborate process which begins with asking your lender for the modification packet and then filling it out and returning it with all the required paperwork. It then requires numerous follow up phone calls and mailings of additional or missing documents to compete the application. You must be aggressive and persistent. The most frustrating part of the modification process is by far the uncertainty of the outcome. Even under a temporary payment plan or trial period, you are not truly sure if you will qualify or be approved until you receive a final letter of approval. This can take countless months and the results can be exacerbating. Many families will apply multiple times before approval or simply giving up.

Whether or not to hire a modification company is another difficult question. Although there are many fine modification companies and professionals out there, whether you can find the right one is another question. The pervasive fraud and poor performance of some modification companies has led a few Attorney Generals to set up websites and laws regarding what fees can be charged and what representations can be made. As with all industries, there are both excellent and poor companies in the mix and because of the sheer desperation of the homeowner, it has opened the area up to some predators. Sometimes a quick internet search of a company name along with the word complaints can be quite revealing. I have performed this type of search in various industries for clients and sometimes instantly discovered vast complaints against a subject business. This is certainly a starting point in researching a business you are considering using. Have you heard the saying that a good salesman can sell you anything? I have and I have been sold. Meaning a good salesperson who tells you what you want to hear can sell you anything, so be careful. Don't hire a company based on a salesperson's representations alone, as we know that if they tell you what you want to hear you may be sold without any true chance of success. Snake oil in the old west was sold the same way as a "cure all". If the sales pitch is too good to be true and seems overly optimistic, beware and check it out. You want confidence and results but if every house was saved so easily, the line would be out the door and the news would be in front. Jesus had 5,000 to feed because he had results and a mob following his every step. Well what if you don't have the funds for a modification company or you simply don't know who to use. You may be best served working aggressively on your own modification through your lender. Unless, of course, you feel confident that the modification company you make contact with is going to do more than hire an $8.00 an hour employee to pacify your questions while they charge you thousands for the service.

At a minimum, do your research on the company, get references and check with your state Attorney General's website for warnings or complaints. I have been contacted a number of times by new clients who were notified by their modification company the day before their home was to be sold at auction, informing them to contact a bankruptcy attorney. Not the kind of service and result they were hired for at best! As with all businesses, there are excellent modification companies and professionals out there; whether you can find one is another question.

Short Sales

What is a short sale? Simply put, a short sale is a sale of real estate in which the mortgage company agrees to accept less than what it is actually owed. The payoff to your mortgage company is therefore short, i.e. less than, what you actually owe them. Therefore, this type of transaction is called a short sale. To achieve a short sale, you will need a contract offer on your home from a buyer which is approved by your current mortgage holder. The transaction is typically coordinated by your realtor, attorney and title company. The approval process, requirements and time frame will vary from mortgage company to mortgage company. One factor you will want to consider is what the taxable effect the short sale will have upon you. The portion of the payoff that is short is typically going to be categorized as loan forgiveness and result in a 1099 being issued to you. You will want to speak with a CPA to determine if the short sale will affect your taxes. The approval process itself can take some time, and that can profoundly affect the success of the sale as well. Some banks will give conditional approvals, such as requiring a seller to bring money to the table to complete the deal. If the amount requested is small, it may be worth considering; but large promissory notes and repayment promises may completely defeat any benefit which would have been derived and may actually result in a less favorable outcome than a foreclosure.

A short sale may also result in some uncertainty as some lenders may not make it clear as to whether or not they will later pursue or bill you for a deficiency. This is the type of transaction where it pays to consult both a tax accountant and an attorney.

Deed In Lieu

A deed in lieu of a foreclosure is a streamlined approach to dealing with the foreclosure process. If the bank agrees, the borrower simply executes a quitclaim deed transferring the property back to the bank; and the need for the foreclosure is then obviated. Ownership of the property passes to the bank, and each party moves on. You will, however, want to consult with your tax professional over what the possible tax effects might be. Although it seems like the obvious solution, many lenders resist the idea of a deed in lieu in favor of the tried and true method of foreclosure. The reasons for this hesitancy can be varied, but the typical roadblocks to "deeds in lieu" are second mortgages, liens and judgments, as these complications can sometimes only be overcome by the traditional foreclosure process. If available, a deed in lieu may be preferential, but always consult first with an attorney and tax accountant before signing any paperwork.

Chapter 13 Bankruptcy

A Chapter 13 bankruptcy is a tremendous and powerful tool and option in stopping a foreclosure sale. Simply put, a chapter 13 bankruptcy filing stops a State foreclosure case in favor of allowing a three to five year repayment plan. The bankruptcy case must be filed prior to a home's sale in foreclosure. The bankruptcy Court appoints a Trustee over each case to review the debtor's qualifications and proposed payment plan. A payment plan would typically take your normal monthly payment and add an additional payment toward arrearages and fees. It may also allow for lien stripping, which is the removal or "stripping" of a second mortgage off a property where the first mortgage consumes all the equity in the home. As the law is ever evolving and proposed legal changes to the Chapter 13 provisions and code are ongoing, it is imperative that you consult with an experienced bankruptcy attorney if you think that bankruptcy is right for you.

    A Chapter 13 bankruptcy can sometimes offer options and possibilities to those in seemingly impossible situations. The bankruptcy Court, Judges and Trustees are sympathetic to the debtor's plight and administer the bankruptcy laws and rules in a way which helps facilitate qualifying individuals to keep their homes. Whether you qualify or not will depend on a number of factors, such as income, expenses and the actual debts to be paid. Some individuals and couples may find that they qualify but that the plan payments are simply too high to be affordable. The plan payment will typically require a high percentage of disposable income to be used toward debt payments and that can sometimes leave the debtor very little leeway in paying other expenses.

    The traditional Ch. 13 bankruptcy helped most in situations where an individual had equity in their home which they wanted to protect, but had fallen behind on their mortgage payments because of a temporary lost job or temporary reduction in income.
A bankruptcy would then allow them to catch up over a period of time and get back on track. Modern bankruptcies are encountering more families with zero to negative equity and permanently lost jobs and reduced income. This is a tough fit as you can't put a round peg in

a square hole. Even for a Ch. 13 bankruptcy to work, you have to have enough income to meet minimum plan requirements as the secured creditor on a first mortgage must get paid to keep your home.

As with any legal option, you have to first do your homework and then get the best advice available to you. Pray for wisdom in decision making, I do. Solomon prayed for wisdom and the Lord opened an abundance to him the likes of which I dare say had never been seen before or after his time.

God's Response to Solomon's Prayer for Wisdom

I will do what you have asked. I will give you a wise and discerning heart, so that there will never have been anyone like you, nor will there ever be. Moreover, I will give you what you have not asked for—both wealth and honor—so that in your lifetime you will have no equal among kings.

1 Kings 3:12-13 NIV

What beautiful words! Just reading God's response to Solomon's prayer for wisdom shows God's almighty power and goodness in response to a prayer from the heart. Pray to God from your heart and he will show you how you should proceed.

Lesson Learned

Whether or not you're at fault in your foreclosure experience, take it as an experience to learn from. What are you learning and what wisdom have you gained?
You are learning to live within your means and preferably under your means. Calculate your living expenses and budget carefully before you rent or buy your next home. When you look for a home or apartment to rent or buy, rent or buy one step under your means. What is one step? It will vary based on your income but let's say a few hundred dollars less a month for a rental and $30,000 to $50,000 less than what you could actually afford for a purchase. This at least gives you a benchmark. If you can afford $1500 a month, try to spend no more than $1200 a month and so on. If a $1000 monthly payment is your limit, try to keep your payment close to $800. It is a wonderful thing to have a little extra money each month and quite a stressful thing to be put out of your home. Enough said, lesson learned.

CHAPTER 15

Crisis Management 101

> LORD my God, I take refuge in you; save and deliver me from all who pursue me,
> Psalm 7:1 NIV

After dealing with thousands of families in distress over the years, the first thing I would tell anyone in a financial crisis, especially a Christian, is to relax. There are no debtor's prisons and no judges who will be yelling at you; undoing financial burdens is pretty much all about money and paperwork. In a sense, even though a foreclosure deals with the single largest debt you will ever owe--your mortgage, even this financial entanglement is mostly a pile of paperwork which, after all is said and done, may seem to dissipate. So for those experiencing a crisis in their finances, take heart, trust God and use the principles in this book as a guide to start you on your way to debt freedom.

So does God care if you're in trouble? Has he left you because you've made some poor choices? Will he still help you if you seek him out? What if you went overboard in spending and were foolish? The Bible's answer is overwhelmingly clear; he does care and he will never leave us nor forsake us.

> Keep your lives free from the love of money and be content with what you have, because God has said, "Never will I leave you; never will I forsake you."
>
> Hebrews 13:5 NIV

God's Word is full of verses that repeatedly carry the theme that God cares deeply about his people, knowing full well their imperfection. If only we had listened to this admonition to be content with what we had, we wouldn't be in this predicament. The problem is, however, that we live in a world of "buy it now and pay for it later." The problem with "pay for it later" is always the same; "later" comes sooner than you think. What happens when you've reached that critical state where your enemies (creditors) are closing in fast? What happens when the creditors are calling you day and night, or you get that knock on the door, serving you with a lawsuit that gives you just twenty days to respond?

Well don't hide your head in the sand and hope the problem goes away. You are going to have to pray for wisdom and then start taking some action. Here is my golden rule for crisis management, "Develop an informed and planned course of action." The rule has two parts. First, get information. Second, plan a course of action.

You're going to want to be proactive. What if you're beyond coming up with a simple budgeting plan and are already in the throws of a lawsuit, foreclosure or a bombardment of collection calls? Where do you go when you are sick? You go to the doctor when you're sick. Where do you go when you're sued? You go to a lawyer when you're sued and that's not rocket science. That's just common sense. Remember, first you need to get information and determine your rights and options. The small amount of money you will spend on an initial consultation will be well worth getting you up to speed with time frames, risks, options and your exposure to liability. Once you have that information, then you can work on a planned course of action. You will want to work toward a solution, a viable solution. You must look realistically at your situation and determine where you want to be and how you can get there. Whatever you do, don't hide your head like an ostrich and pretend that it will all go away. Remember, the goal of this text is to get you out of debt, not to delay and ignore what's going on around you. While you're hiding your head, the creditor and their attorney are planning their next move. The good thing is that you already know what they want—money. The bad thing is that you may not have any money to give them. So what do you do?

A Christian in crisis needs a plan just like the creditor has a plan. The Lord has a plan for your life and it's not to be in debt forever. The creditor also has its own plan for each defaulted loan. They don't just wing it; they know exactly what they are going to do. Their goal is to get your money into their pocket. How they achieve this goal likely involves a fairly detailed and well thought out course of action. In order to formulate your ideal plan, you should be somewhat familiar with what their plan may look like. Only then will you understand the importance of having a defensive plan of action.

> "Settle matters quickly with your adversary who is taking you to court. Do it while you are still together on the way, or your adversary may hand you over to the judge, and the judge may hand you over to the officer, and you may be thrown into prison.
>
> Matthew 5:25 NIV

The Creditor's Plan

The creditor's plan to collect on your debt may look something like this:

1. Send monthly billing statement to debtor.

2. If overdue, charge a late fee (extra revenue).

3. If overdue again, raise interest rate (more revenue).

4. If still overdue, send a letter of default.

5. A month later, turn over to a collection company.

6. At three to six months overdue, turn over to an attorney.

7. Send final letter of demand prior to filing suit.

8. File lawsuit or foreclosure.

9. Obtain judgment and or sale date.

10. Sell home for foreclosures/garnish wages for judgments.

11. For foreclosures, issue 1099 or pursue deficiency judgment/For regular judgments, seize and search for assets.

Steven Cohen

Wow, think of the detailed plans creditors have just to collect from you. They must have a clear plan when they are dealing repeatedly with overdue debts. You're fighting a debt war and you can't be idle; and you can't be without a counteroffensive strategy. You must take action and be ready now, not later. While it may seem overwhelming, there are quite a few options out there; and hope for your future is something you can bank on with God's help. Although there are no debtor's prisons in the United States, the book of Matthew gives a wise admonition to the debtor. i.e. settle on your way to court as stated in Matthew 5:25. Remember, you can get out of debt; you can overcome. Down on your luck doesn't mean out of luck. It's just a temporary setback and you're going to get out of it but you have to work on it. How many times in the Bible did God's people face overwhelming forces, yet win? The key to success was to be strong in the Lord and to have a plan of action.

Different situations will require different plans. Here is a sample plan to get you started. We will also look in detail at different types of crises which you may face and how to prepare effectively.

May the LORD answer you when you are in distress; may the name of the God of Jacob protect you.
       Psalm 20:1 NIV

May he give you the desire of your heart
and make all your plans succeed.

       Psalm 20:4 NIV

This is your Plan for Credit Card Debts

1. Pray for wisdom in all decision making. One of my most impossible cases ever was solved at mediation after I prayed to the Lord to let it be settled.
   It was such an A to Z change; it had to be from God.
2. No new charges; if you're in debt, it's time to pay for all purchases in cash.
3. Always make on time payments and pay at least the minimum; if all you can pay is the minimum payment, realize that you're in trouble!
4. Set up a budget to knock out your bills in at least 3 to 5 years; keep track of all balances, interest rates and due dates on a spreadsheet.
5. Get excited about working down debt, it's your new goal.
6. If you're in default, contact your creditor to try and negotiate a low lump sum payment like 50 % to settle the debt. Borrow from your family if you can.
7. If you can't make a lump sum payment, try to negotiate a payment plan with no interest accruing while you're paying it back.
8. If you're sued, immediately consult with an attorney.
9. Negotiate a payment plan and place it into your monthly budget.
10. If no payment plan is viable and you're in great debt, consult with a bankruptcy attorney to determine if a Ch. 7 bankruptcy, meaning one that would wipe out all your credit cards to zero, is an option.

Let's look at some of the plans various components. Many debtors make the mistake of seeing an attorney far too late in the debt collection process. If you've been sued, you need to quickly assess your legal rights, options for settlement, liability, and exposure to future collection. An initial consultation can provide you with invaluable information as to where you stand, your risks and what you should be doing. The legal window opens and closes very quickly with heavy results, so don't wait. You should also see an accountant. Why see an accountant too? A good accountant can also assist you in evaluating your financial picture and whether or not you're beyond financial repair and a candidate for bankruptcy. The attorney can guide you in this determination as well; however, a consultation with each professional can shed greater light on the direction you should be heading. Remember, this is "crisis management"; and when you're sued, you're in a crisis. While this crisis is not an insolvable predicament, it is one that should be dealt with immediately so that your future recovery is not delayed.

The importance of a budget to your financial future and plan cannot be stressed enough. Without a budget, you will likely never get out of debt and never be protected from getting back into debt. Few to none of my former bankruptcy clients ever operated off of a regular monthly budget. Simply put, a budget is a plan for how you will spend and save the money coming in each month. Once you have a budget, review it each month and use it to start wisely managing your income and expenses. Even if you are far out of alignment, a budget is critical as it will help you determine where you stand financially and it will also let you see where you need to be. A budget is also a reality check with your current situation. To many, a budget may seem childish, but every corporation in America and virtually every church operates off a budget. Without one, you're spending and finances will be in chaos. Ask the most successful person you know if they operate off a budget and you'll be surprised at the answer. It will most likely be "Of course I do."

With your budget in place, you can now determine what, if anything, you can plan to pay toward the debt being collected upon. Many suits can be settled quickly with a payment plan. Remember, you already know what they are after—money; you just need to determine if you have enough to make a payment; and if not, you need to figure out what your options are. If you can make a payment, contact the creditor and see what can be arranged. Obviously you're trying for a low payment, and they are trying for a high payment. You may also be able to make a lump sum payment to settle the debt. Creditors will vary on what they will accept in settlement. Some may drop the bill 15% to 20%, while others may take up to 50% off and even a few much more. This might be a good time to contact your parents or a friend for some financial help or a friendly loan. Owing your parents is certainly better than owing the creditor's attorney. Whatever you work out, get it in writing and make sure you read carefully anything you sign.

You're planning to settle any debt has to be realistic. In determining whether or not you can make payments on your debts, you will generally want to ask yourself the following question: Can I come up with a written plan to get out of debt in three to five years? If you roll your eyes at that question, you may be a candidate for a bankruptcy. Even though bankruptcy is not what one plans for, if you're debt is wildly out of control then it may be an option you need to consider. Bankruptcy can be an important tool in your arsenal of debt defense options and is one method of becoming debt free. The Bible speaks of the year of jubilee in the book of Deuteronomy. This was a provision to provide for debt relief every seven years in an attempt to end slavery and unrelenting servitude over debt.

What if you truly can't afford any payment and your debts are out of control? First, you are not alone. Many people only discover their dire situation at the point of no return. If you are so overwhelmed that you can't get back on track and you feel the world is closing in on you, it's time to look at a possible Ch. 7 bankruptcy. Basically, a Chapter 7 bankruptcy is a declaration that you have no viable ability to pay back your debts and it wipes most debts out in a period of a few months. Most secured debts like mortgages, car loans, etc. do not get erased unless you surrender the assets to which they are linked. A Chapter 13 bankruptcy, which involves a 3 to 5 year payment plan, is a more elaborate bankruptcy option which is geared more to those in foreclosure trouble who don't want to lose their home or for those with great income, great debt and great problems paying those debts. Bankruptcy is a vital relief valve for those in overwhelming financial crisis.

It's a merciful option for those in way over their heads and who need a fresh start. Whether or not you qualify is more complex than just how much money you make. It involves calculations and comparisons in what is called the "Means Test." This test determines if you qualify under the federal guidelines. Only an experienced bankruptcy attorney can truly make that determination.

Foreclosures

Well, what if you're in or close to foreclosure and you don't know what to do?

You're going to have to keep a few things in mind. First, Rome was not concurred in a day and your mortgage woes will also not be solved in a day. It may take many months of steadfast determination and repeated attempts at modification or resolution to get anything accomplished. In addition to praying for wisdom in the situation you are going to want to access some professionals. First, you will want to speak with an attorney in your State and County to get some general information regarding: a) The time a foreclosure takes in your jurisdiction b) Possible options c) Possible liabilities. In some locals a foreclosure may take close to a year while in others in may proceed like a rocket.

If you are not comfortable with the information provided, get a second opinion as gathering information is your cheapest best first step. Second, you will want to speak with a certified public accountant regarding possible tax issues. Within a foreclosure you will hear and be dealing with a number of terms, such as short sale, deed in lieu of foreclosure and modification. Each of these may or may not have a tax implication and you need to be aware of them. A short sale (a sale in which the bank accepts less than the full amount due on the mortgage) may result in a 1099 being issued to you for debt forgiveness; a deed in lieu of foreclosure (where the bank takes the property back by deed and skips foreclosing) may also have a tax implication as may a straight foreclosure where the lender could choose to forgive the unpaid balance and issue you a 1099 as well. How the 1099 affects your income taxes will vary based on the tax laws at the time and whether or not the property was a primary residence or an investment property. Need I say more; you need to speak with an accountant. The third professional you will want to speak with is a mortgage broker. In some instances, you may have enough equity for a traditional refinance which could bring you back to a current status. Also, with ever changing laws and loan programs being offered, you want to make sure you have exhausted all possibilities and not missed out on any new options.

As you deal with a foreclosure crisis, you are going to have to ask yourself some tough questions. You may not want to hear it, but you're also going to have to deal with reality, not fantasy. First, should you be even trying to keep your home or is it just too far upside down for you to ever make it work? Second, can you even afford the home if it were brought current or modified? Third, where will you and your home's value be in 5 to 10 years? For example, a person earning $35,000 a year just can't afford a $200,000 home. This is not negativity, it's just plain reality. An income of $35,000 a year is designed for a low cost home or townhome and would probably be stretched keeping a home of $70,000 to $80,000; so how on earth is a $200,000 to $250,000 home even a remote possibility. Current loan modification options will generally look to either a government backed plan or a lenders in house plan, but both have to deal with the income and expense reality of the borrower making the application. When a lender reviews a loan modification application, they are looking at income and expenses based on a number of preset ratios. This examination compares income and current expenses in relation to the loan which must be maintained. If all your income is consumed by your normal monthly living expenses before you get to the mortgage payment, it's just not going to work. You are going to have to take a realistic look at your both your financial situation and your home's value, now and in the future to determine if staying put is really in your best interest. Although it is not good to default on your debts, if your home is $100,000 to $200,000 upside down and you can't afford it anyway, a foreclosure may be a blessing in disguise. Well, with all that said, what follows is a basic plan and a starting point to deal with a foreclosure:

Steven Cohen

This is Your Plan for Foreclosures

1. Pray for guidance and wisdom including not just "how to keep your home," but also "whether or not you should keep your home."
2. If served with foreclosure papers, consult with an attorney immediately.
3. Speak with a tax professional so that you know where you stand in regards to the different options you may be offered such as a short sale, deed in lieu of foreclosure, etc.
4. Speak with a mortgage broker to see if a traditional refinance is an option.
5. Prepare a monthly budget to see whether or not you can afford the home with or without a modification.
6. Immediately apply for a modification, keep copies of all documents you send in and regularly follow up with your lender.
7. Don't wait. If you know what you need to do, do it and get the clock started as there are a lot of people in line. E.g. If you know you need to sell your home, put it on the market now.
8. Don't waste your stay. If you're not making a monthly mortgage payment, save your money each month so that you have money to move or negotiate a resolution at the end of the process.
9. Negotiate a payment plan and place it into your monthly budget.
10. If there are no viable options, consider filing a Ch. 7 or Ch. 13.

CHAPTER 16

Financial Management 101

Lesson 1: Debt freedom takes planning.

You might think that an attorney dealing with so many people facing mountains of debt might be tired of going over all those numbers, all those budgets and all those financial plans which went awry. What financial plans? What budgets? What numbers that went awry? While the bank and credit card companies are operating off a detailed budget and complex financial model worked out by experienced accountants, you're being told to "buy now and pay it off later." You're being told "no interest for a year." You're being told "on sale today only." WHAT? Where's your financial plan, your budget, your financial model? THERE ISN'T ONE, IS THERE? If you had one, you would be sitting pretty good right now. Does anybody care about your financial model or whether your family can afford the purchase? NO. I think not. Well I'm generalizing of course, but you get the general idea. A grocery store sells both healthy and fattening foods, but it's up to you to choose wisely. No one follows you down the aisle at the store and says, "I don't think you need those extra cupcakes." You have to control yourself and the same is true with credit cards and debt. You have to protect yourself from becoming overextended. Was "Personal Financial Management" or "Budgeting 101" on your high school's list of electives? I wish it were. Even if a high school was wise enough to offer such a class, why would such a necessary life skill not be required as mandatory to a student's primary education? How can you go through twelve to fifteen or more years of school and never have a class on budgeting and personal finance? It seems preposterous, but I think I never had such a class. Sounds a little crazy but that's the world we live in and that's what we have to deal with.

Planning quite simply starts with a monthly budget. Most bills are paid monthly and a monthly budget gives you a regular chance to look at your finances on a regular basis. A monthly budget also gives you an opportunity to incrementally, i.e. monthly, improve your situation by increasing your savings and decreasing your debt, because that is the main goal. Your budget's main purpose is to allow you to monitor whether you're going in the right direction, meaning savings up, and debt down. It also allows you to provide for discretionary spending. If you want to make a larger purchase, budget it. It may not be fun to wait an extra four months to buy a TV, but it sure beats having to get up during your favorite show to answer a rude collection call because you couldn't afford it in the first place.

Lesson 2: A ship without a course runs aground as quickly as a person without a budget goes broke.

If you are operating without a budget, you are sailing your financial ship without any course, and you are not alone. Virtually everyone who is over their head in debt shares a common thread. No course. No budget. No financial plan for the future. I don't mean they never made a budget, I mean they failed to operate off a monthly budget which considered their income and expenses. If they did have a budget, they failed to stick to it and soon fell back on the old pattern of *buy whatever you want, whenever you want.* There is also another common thread among most of those in great debt; they never really evaluated their purchases in terms of what they could actually afford. This sensible logic sounds so basic, yet it is almost universally ignored. When you ask someone if they have a budget, you often get the kind of look that says, "I'm no child, and I don't need a budget to know what I can afford." Oh yes you do! Do you think your church could operate without a budget? Well, churches trust on the Lord for their income, but they also very carefully plan out their budgets. When donations run short, they adjust their budget to meet the shortfall, and they try and raise additional funds to compensate. God's provisions are precious and we must carefully plan their use. Budgeting is not child's play; it's a modern day necessity.

Repeat after me, "I will operate off a budget." If you and your family budget, you will prosper and eventually get out of debt. If you don't, your future will hold endless harassing phone calls, stressful nights, arguments and the like. If you are in a financial crisis, you have likely not been operating off a budget and making financial decisions based on that budget. Now there are many causes for financial crisis, like loosing one's job, illness and family tragedy. These unpredictable misfortunes can throw even the best financial strategist into turmoil. However, a good budget will help you prepare for the bad times as well as the good times.

In over fifteen years of legal practice, debt defense and bankruptcy law, I have yet to meet someone that says, "I have been operating off of this written budget for the last year, and I don't understand what went wrong." It's simply not the case among those in financial trouble. It's more often the case that the first true budget is drawn up on the way to the attorney's office or on a visit to the accountant to see what went wrong.

What if God had no plan for your future? No plan to defeat Satan? No plan for salvation? No plan for forgiveness of sins? Can you imagine if Jesus had not spoken of his return, his resurrection, a new heaven and a new earth, and everlasting life. Jesus was the planed sacrifice for our sins, the payment--in full—for our debts. Without God's beautiful plan of Christ and his written word of salvation, we would be like ships without a rudder. God does not operate without a plan nor does any wise steward. If God has so carefully laid out the plan for our salvation and our future from the foundations of the World, shouldn't we then also plan out our lives and what we will do with the finances with which we have been entrusted?

The Concept behind your budget

Before you start a budget and construct a financial plan, you must understand the concepts behind them. You have to start thinking of yourself as a steward of your own business. The business is yourself and your work fuels that business. Your business generates income each month and, over the course of your lifetime, will likely generate more than a million dollars of revenue. You, therefore, are a million dollar business and God has put you in charge of your funds. We are each then millionaires; we just don't get all the money to work with at the same time. If you're a wise steward and operate your business within your budget, you will have extra savings. If you operate your business over budget, you will be in debt.

At this point, it is more likely than not that you have been operating over budget. This overspending has to stop and you have to do two things: First, stop the bleeding, meaning stop spending more than you earn. Second, start knocking down your debt through a progressive repayment plan. By progressive, I mean you keep at it. You may have to start a little slow, but as your budget and planning progress, your expenses will be reduced and you will be able to knock off more and more debt. The path to debt freedom occurs in stages. Different categories of debts will require different lengths of time to reach the payoff goal. You hold the keys to debt reduction. Each sacrifice you make and each incremental step you take toward knocking out your debt will increase the rate at which your debt is paid off. One thing is for certain, if you start paying down your debts, you will start seeing and feeling a difference in your financial future.

Let's get organized

You may be saying, "Well, what's the plan because I'm in trouble?" Ok, one step at a time. First, you must be organized. Before you can know where you're going, you have to know where you are. Do you know how much you owe? I don't mean approximately; I mean exactly? Do you know how much interest you're paying each month? How many late fees, over-the-limit fees, etc., you are incurring? These fees have to stop and minimum payments need to be resumed. Your credit card's balances need to start going down—even if slowly—not up. What are the interest rates for each card you're carrying? You need to know this because it's your money and each dollar you save or eliminate from expenses can be applied to debt reduction. Would you like to borrow $500 at 18% interest, 28% interest? No, of course not! But wait, that's what you've done if you have credit card debt and you need to know exactly what you're paying. Why, because you want to shift that debt from high interest payments to low interest payments to no interest payments. It's almost impossible to get out of debt, if the rate you're paying is out of hand. You need to know exactly what each card is costing you so that you can focus on the high rates first, eliminate them and then move on.

  So pull out your pen and paper or turn on your computer and let's get a spreadsheet started. From now on, when someone says how much do you owe? You are going to say "$23,124 or $55,410 or $3,212." When someone says, "What do you make?" you will say "$42,000 or $27,000 or $143,000." The old you is history; the new you is on top of your finances. Once you take charge, good things are going to start happening. The interest and fees you're paying are real, and you need to have a month-to-month gauge of how much your credit is costing you. Only then can you start working on reducing them, even if slowly at first. You need to get excited about seeing those debts decrease, those rates go down, and those bills disappear. Remember, once you pay off your credit card that's costing you $50 a month in interest, that $50 a month goes back into your pocket or your savings account.

A budget is a debtor's best friend

When you look back in a few years, you will hug your budget, kiss it, and put it under your pillow. Well, that may be a little extreme but you know what I mean. A well planned budget can and will be your financial best friend. Ignore it and trouble waits. Have fun with it and you will reap what you sow, meaning savings and eventual debt freedom. You see the budget is your guide map to decision making, your gas gauge, and your GPS device. Don't fight it, use it, and thrive within it. How do you make a budget? It's not hard at all, and it's something you will tinker with each month like a professional race car driver who is trying to get every bit of speed out of his race car. The basic idea is to start with your net income at the top and then to list out all your bills, expenses, debt payments, savings, tithes and allocations you will make during the month with the goal of not spending more than you make. What if you are spending more then you make? Well, you are not a sovereign nation which can print money, so you will have to reduce expenses, increase income or both. Below you will find a sample budget to start with, but you will have to fill in your own numbers. It is designed to give some basic guidelines, suggestions and guidance to those seeking to get out of or avoid debt crisis. The suggestions, limits and recommendations in this sample budget are based on rates and amounts which I have found seem to place families at risk of default and which are made to try and guide you. There is also some guidance as to *how much is too much* and *when is enough,*

enough. The **<** **(less than)** symbol on the suggested budget worksheet means just that; seek to keep your payments or percentage **less than** the suggested amount or work toward that goal. These formulas are based on amounts and interest rates which I have seen lead many families into trouble over the years. So if you're paying more than the **<(less than)** interest rate, you may be in a little trouble and you need to try and work toward a lower interest rate or payment in the future. The "No add'l purchases" (no additional purchases) notation is based on the idea that if you have a second mortgage, second car payment, or $3500 in credit card debt, you need to be focusing on knocking out debt, not incurring new bills. It is a time for sacrifice and conservation, not excesses and additional debt. Luxury items can be reduced or eliminated, and direct control items can be managed and reduced to a degree.

A Sample Monthly Budget

(PLUSES +)
Net Income: $_____
Additional Income: $_____

(Minuses -)   HOME & CAR
Mortgage (Rent): $_____ <7%
Add'l Principal Pmt. $_____ (Try to pay off in 20 years or less)
2nd Mortgage: $_____ <8% (No add'l purchases until knocked out)
Add'l Principal Pmt: $_____ (Try to pay off in 10 years or less)
HOA fees: $_____
Car 1 $_____ <$450   Rate<9.5%
Car 2 $_____ <$375   Rate<9.5% (No add'l purchases until knocked out)

(Minuses -)   UTILITIES
Electric (gas) $_____ <$250
Water $_____ <$80
Telephone $_____ <$125
Cell Phone $_____ <$100 (Luxury)
Cable/Satellite $_____ <$75 (Luxury)

(Minuses-)   INSURANCE AND MAINTENANCE
Insurance Total $_____ (Car:_____ Home:_____ Life:_____)
                             Annual review for rates
Gasoline $_____ <300 (Direct control) Get a fuel efficient car.

                 OTHER BILLS
Student Loans $_____ (Balance $_____/120) (10 year repayment plan)
Tithes/Charity $_____   10% goal
Savings/Retirement $_____   10% goal
Food $_____ <$500 (Direct Control: varies by family size)

             DEBT RETIREMENT   (<12.5%)   Can also use: /12 (1 yr)
Credit Card 1: $_____ (Avg. balance_____/36)   /24 (2 yr)
                                       % Rate:_____   up to /60 (5 yr)
Credit Card 2: $_____ (Avg. balance_____/36)
                                         % Rate:_____
Credit Card 3: $_____ (Avg. balance_____/36)
                                         % Rate:_____
Credit Debt 4: $_____ (Avg. balance_____/36)
                                         % Rate:_____
             (No additional purchases if over $3500 in credit card debt)
             (This offers a sample 3 year debt elimination plan)

Total Monthly Expenses: $_____
Difference: $_____ (Income-Expenses)

Copyright 2011. All rights reserved

Reducing Expenses

There are basically two ways you can go about reducing your monthly expenses. You can either increase your monthly income or reduce your monthly costs or both. We will look at reducing expenses first. The largest and longest term expense you will typically deal with is your home, which is why it is so important to keep your monthly housing payments low, with the goal of paying the loan off sooner rather than later. Adding a little extra each month can go a long way in speeding up your mortgage payoff date by years and effectively reducing the amount of your debt considerably. If you are able, put your mortgage on a spreadsheet and keep track of how you are doing. It can be quite fun to see the large effect of a small amount of extra money added to principal each month. Well what about the here and now? Your interest rate controls your current monthly payment, and reducing it should always be in the back of your mind. Be vigilant and patiently look for the right opportunity to refinance at a better rate. If that it not an option, and you feel overwhelmed by your home payment, you may wish to try and sell your home to move to something more affordable with a lower monthly payment. If none of these options are available, then look to other expenses to reduce your costs. Utilities are far overlooked as an adjustable expense. Yes, we all need water and electricity, but you may be able to reduce some of your utility bills just the same. Typically, an air conditioner and heater create the largest demand on your electric bill. Setting the thermostat a few degrees warmer or cooler may make a $25 to $75 a month difference and that adds up. Also, there are now energy efficient light bulbs which take only one quarter of the electricity to run. Are you getting the idea? Look at your electric bill and you can likely reduce it through a little effort and probably very little discomfort. The same can be said of your phone and cable bill. If you have financial problems, you need to work at it from all angles. You can do with a little less cable service, if it means less collection calls and a brighter future. Remember, every dollar you spend today must be paid back tomorrow. Reduced bills and expenses are just as good as savings and increased income. You can put off that new car purchase a few more months or even a year; you can live with a little less, especially if you are in crisis or are trying to avoid one. Once you decide to reduce expenses and focus on saving as opposed to spending, it will be easy to find new ways to reduce your bills.

Increasing Income

Earning more money can be a tremendous help in dealing with a financial crisis. At a certain point it may be time for a spouse to return to the workforce or for you to take on a night job. Even a low paying job as a clerk can make a difference. A little extra income can cover an electric bill or a car bill, and this type of proactive action can help you avoid default. Sometimes additional income is the only short term solution to meet monthly bills. If you're in a low income position, you should be looking for ways to advance your position, either through education or promotion. Look at job openings within the company your currently at to see if additional training or degrees can increase your income level. A worker may spend twenty to forty years in the workforce which is why it is important to have short term and long term goals. Because of the longevity of your working career, it may never be too late to go back to school or to try new things. Pray for God's wisdom and guiding hand and he will bless what you do. If you do go back to school, have a plan, not just a student loan to pay. That is to say, there are certain jobs and occupations you can train for that you know will have a decent wage an a likely job waiting for you. One example might be nursing where there is a demand for skilled labor and paying jobs typically available. Be realistic and err on the side of caution when it comes to incurring more student loans. Do not throw darts in the dark, but do your research and be aware of the job market out there and real job openings which you feel you can or would be able to fill with proper training.

Monthly Review and Family Meetings

A budget, especially for a family, is a team effort. If married, you should partner with your spouse and review your budget each month. The Bible seems fairly clear in its teaching that you should not be enslaved to debt. I have dealt with moms and dads who were still paying their child's phone bill in spite of being on the brink of bankruptcy. There is a time when even parents have to ask their adult children for help and, at least, in a sensible and appropriate way, let their adult children know that they have to cut down on expenses. Children are resilient and can be supportive in times of limited finances. It can be a time of character building and trusting the Lord. We all want to give our children everything we can; however, if you're getting four collection calls a day, the cable and extra cell phone may have to go. It may also be an ideal time for your son or daughter, of appropriate age, to get their first job at the local grocery store so that they can learn some personal responsibility and have some funds to pay for their own cell phone or to use as discretionary spending money.

CHAPTER 17

Is there a heavenly 401k plan?

> "But store up for yourselves treasures in heaven, where moths and vermin do not destroy, and where thieves do not break in and steal."
>
> Matthew 6:20 NIV

It's amazing how we can be so willing to pay 15-29% interest on a flat screen television placed on a credit card, yet so coldly tremble when it comes to giving our money to the church or a ministry. Don't you realize that God owns everything and if the streets of heaven are made of purest gold and the new Jerusalem's foundation is decorated with every kind of precious stone, that there is going to be plenty left over for us. The simplest answer to whether there is a heavenly 401k plan that we can contribute to is *YES*. Matthew 6:20-21 lays it out beautifully, with a direction, a reason and a justification.

First, there is a reward for tithing, meaning giving to the church, the poor and the Lord's work in general. You will be storing up treasure for yourself in heaven, our final destination for eternity. Think of it as a heavenly

401k plan. It's not fiction or a joke; it's a promise written in God's Word. Jesus also made mention of such a wonderful future in his own words in the book of John.

> My Father's house has many rooms; if that were not so, would I have told you that I am going there to prepare a place for you?
>
> John 14:2 NIV

The Lord wants what's best for us as we are his children and he refers to himself as our heavenly father. There is clearly a reward, a treasure if you will, for giving the tithe. That is, it will be recorded by God and apparently credited to us in heaven. God doesn't need our money, but he does want our hearts and devotion. If you are focused on giving to God and surrendering to the Lord's will, your heart will be centered on the Lord and his heavenly kingdom, which is where the Lord wants us to store our treasure. Do you have to give? Of course not, as giving is a voluntary act which shows our willingness to serve God and our fellow man. The encouragement that I give to you is that your funds will not be wasted as they apparently will be stored in heaven. Even better is the fact that we apparently will be rewarded directly in heaven for our giving. It is certainly a nice thought to realize that your gifts are being stored in heaven as a reward.

What if I'm broke and I can't even pay my current bills? The Lord will watch over you and he knows your heart. Jesus remarked lovingly about the widow that gave the smallest donation possible, a mite. Although this might have only been a few pennies, it was all she had and she will be remembered for all eternity for her gift. Certainly others gave more that day, but hers was from the heart. There are families out there making over a hundred thousand dollars a year saying, "We can't afford to give to the church." There are also families making $35,000 a year that are giving.

Make giving something a priority or at least a goal in your budget and you will be blessed. Do you know that even the U.S. bankruptcy code allows for debtors to use regular and continued charitable contributions in the calculation as to whether or not they qualify for filing for bankruptcy relief? There are some debtors that, had they tithed, would have qualified for bankruptcy relief, but because they did not give anything to charity, they did not have enough expenses to meet the requirements of the law.

So many families have no clue how much they earn, spend or need each month to live. Giving to the church or a ministry each month can actually have the positive result of helping you budget your funds and can help you focus on what you're earning and what your own needs are. How ironic it is that I can think, "I don't have the money to give to the church", yet I can still stop at a store and consider an expensive purchase in almost the same day. The mind is willing but the body is weak. When it's something we want, the funding is immediately available, and we provide for our own supposed needs by justifying more debt on our credit card. But when it's something God asks from us, and therefore a true need, it is so hard for us to uncurl our fingers from the money he has entrusted to us. Whenever we tithe, we not only give towards the earthly needs of God's people—the Church, *we recognize our need*—to depend on him, to be transformed by him and to invest in God's eternal kingdom.

You must change your way of thinking about the tithe and about giving to the poor and God's work. Think of it as direct heavenly savings, your 401k for after retirement here on earth. As you place the money in the offering plate at church, it's being deposited up above into *your* account. I'm not making that up; I'm quoting the Bible, "Store up for yourselves treasure in heaven." We have seen with the unfortunate nature of the stock market, the real estate market and this economy that there is no guarantee when it comes to money and return on investment. But there is one guaranteed place where your money can never be stolen and where the Lord makes it evident, it will be safe, *heaven*.

In the same way, let your light shine before others, that they may see your good deeds and glorify your Father in heaven.
Matthew 5:16 NIV

We live in a tough world which seems so fixated on money and what it can buy, that we can fail to see the true meaning of life. There is certainly more to life then money, but what you do with your money says a lot about you and it also says a lot about what you believe in and whom you serve. Helping others is never going to be something you'll regret. Giving to your church should never be a painful choice, but one made with the joy and knowledge that you're letting your light shine in doing what is right and that it glorifies God. Remember the parable about the Good Samaritan. The beauty of this story was not only the goodness of the act performed, but the irony surrounding the one who was good. The act of kindness was shown by one whom many, by prejudice, believed could not perform a good act. God affords all of us debtors to his goodness the opportunity to show his goodness, and that only by his grace. As Christians, our deeds, actions and words are always under the microscope of the world. So let your light so shine.

After almost fifteen years of helping those in great financial need, I have yet to see someone who placed themselves into financial crisis by tithing or giving 10% of their income to the church. On the contrary, the wealthiest couple I know gives almost 30% of their monthly income to the church and that still leaves them with enough money to take their favorite attorney to lunch, go figure. They have great faith and I pray the Lord to give such great faith to us all.

What about my earthly retirement plan?

We have talked about heavenly savings, but what about retirement planning and savings in general. Retirement savings is a 10 on a scale of 1 to 10! Retirement savings are generally safe assets as many states protect them from creditor's claims, and they are tax deferred so there is a built-in incentive to save and contribute. Employer matched retirement plans are even better because you may be doubling every dollar you contribute. But what if you have a good amount of retirement savings and are also in a substantial amount of debt?

Should I cash in my earthly retirement plan to pay off my earthly debts?

What about those thinking of cashing in their retirement plans to pay off or catch up with their debts? On a scale of 1-10, that plan hits me as a 1! I have met quite a few people who I wish had spoken with an attorney or accountant prior to their failed attempt to settle their debts by cashing in their retirement. It's not the idea that's bad; it is typically the execution and the result. First, most people who cash in their retirement only solve about half of their problems; that is, they only pay off a portion of their debts leaving more than enough debt to still topple them. Second, many individuals who pay off their debts through cashing in retirement are back into debt a few years later. It is like an alcoholic throwing out all their alcohol and then buying it back a few months later or leaving a few bottles hidden somewhere. If you don't change your spending habits dramatically at the same time you pay off your debts, you won't have the help you need to stay out of debt. Further, the tax hit on cashing in retirement is generally so tremendous that a new debt may be created as well. Whatever the case may be, it is certainly easier to spend than to save; and you can cash in and spend twenty years worth of retirement in about twenty minutes, if you are not careful. If this is still your plan, make sure you have thought it out well in advance so it achieves your goal. Then change your spending habits dramatically for the better.

CHAPTER 18

Plan to win the race to debt freedom

> Do you not know that in a race all the runners run, but only one gets the prize? Run in such a way as to get the prize.
> 1 Corinthians 9:24 NIV

A race? Yes, a race. You are not going to sit back in despair, nor are you going to take it slowly. Now is the time to take action, aggressive and planned action, to curb the situation you're in. In the book of Corinthians, Paul advised believers to live their lives holy to the Lord in the same way as a runner would who was seeking to win a race. We can apply the same fervor and energy in winning the race to becoming debt free and financially independent. Run in such a way as to win the race! One thing is for sure, you are not getting out of debt without a plan to win, and a budget is that plan. Keeping at your budget is your training and if you do so, you will win. I have never met someone in overwhelming debt who said, "I don't know what went wrong; I have been operating on a budget each month." Quite the opposite, those who find themselves drowning in debt are typically only just realizing they are in over their heads when they can no longer pay their bills; and by then, it is a little late in the game. The time to consider the cost and merit of a car purchase is before you go to the dealer, not at the table after you've looked at the car with all the bells and whistles. If you don't plan to win the game of debt with some type of budget, you will lose. But there is no reason to lose, no matter where you currently are. Just start training to win. Every financial decision you make in the future can be referred back to your budget for consideration, to determine if it's within your training plan. The decision of how much to borrow on a home, for example, should not be dependent on how much you can convince a lender to loan you. It should be based on a careful study of your planned budget and what you can truly afford. Just like paying off your credit cards is not going to happen with you sitting at home on the couch with the phone off the hook and the TV on. Plan for success; plan to spend only what is within your budget. With a budget in place, you can pace yourself on the race towards debt freedom. If you start the course and stick with it, you will finish the race. But you must start. Use the budget and principals in this book as a starting point and a guide. If you do, you will start seeing results sooner rather than later. Well, what if you've already made all those ill advised purchases? Rome was not conquered in a day and neither will your debt, but there is a way out and you must start pursuing it. You must operate off of a plan and a budget. If you don't, you're like a ship captain without a wheel and a compass. You will run aground. May the Lord guide you and bless you as you move forward toward debt freedom with the wisdom, guidance and principles offered in this book and in the holiest book of all, the Bible. May you run to win the race.

> "But those who hope in the LORD will renew their strength. They will soar on wings like eagles; they will run and not grow weary, they will walk and not be faint."
>
> Isaiah 40:31 NIV

Author's contact information:
Steven Reed Cohen, Esquire
Fountains Executive Center
9000 W. Sheridan St., Suite 171
Pembroke Pines, FL 33024
(954) 436-9895
srcohenlaw@live.com

Scriptures taken from the Holy Bible, New International Version®, NIV®. Copyright © 1973, 1978, 1984, 2011 by Biblica, Inc.™ Used by permission of Zondervan. All rights reserved worldwide. www.zondervan.com.

www.ingramcontent.com/pod-product-compliance
Lightning Source LLC
Chambersburg PA
CBHW052048070526
44584CB00017B/2106